7-50

Help for the Dyslexic Adolescent

by

E.G. Stirling

Typeset by Folio Photosetting, Bristol
Printed by Antony Rowe Ltd, Chippenham, Wiltshire.

Jacket design by Geoffrey Lincoln

ISBN 0-9512529-0-9

Available from:
E.G. Stirling, 114 Westbourne Rd.,
Sheffield S10 2QT. (0114) 2662286

Contents

Acknowledgements

I would like to acknowledge with gratitude the help and support I received during the writing of this book. In particular, warm thanks are due to:

The Headmaster of St David's College, Llandudno, for his interest and encouragement.

My colleagues in the Dyslexia Unit, U.C.N.W. Bangor, for generously sharing their ideas with me.

Lee Pascal, for permission to adapt and use his test.

Barbara Kinsella, for typing the manuscript.

Alexandra, for careful proofreading.

Charles Stirling, for constant and enthusiastic support,

and finally to Miles, Tom, Edward, Fionan, Toby and Andrew.

'. . . the intolerable wrestle
with words and meanings.'
T.S. Eliot 'East Coker'

For
I.M.S.

Eileen Stirling has been teaching dyslexic children for the past 13 years, initially in the Dyslexia Unit run by T.R. and E. Miles at Bangor, and for the last ten years at St David's College, Llandudno. She gained her M.Ed. (Dyslexia) in 1978, and has given talks to teachers and parents, as well as lecturing on Courses.

Eileen Stirling is also the author of 'Spelling Check-List; a Dictionary for Dyslexics', published by St David's College, Llandudno in 1984 (price £1.25).

Chapter 1

Introduction

Yet another book on dyslexia; that needs some justification. For the past 13 years I have been teaching dyslexic adolescents, and as a result I have been involved in giving talks and lectures to teachers and students. It is striking how many people come up afterwards to ask for names of books or authors dealing with this age group. The answer has had to be that there is in fact very little published material. Most teaching books on dyslexia concentrate on the early stages of the primary school child, where one can confidently begin at the beginning, with short vowel sounds, consonant blends etc, thus building up a safe and reliable structure, unhindered by a mish-mash of already acquired and semi-absorbed 'rules' governing the English language – which is what the typical 13 year old or even 17 year old dyslexic commonly comes equipped with.

I felt therefore that there was a gap to be filled. I claim no originality, and am humbly conscious of the great debt I owe to my colleagues, for sharing their thoughts and ideas with me, and to my pupils, who have taught me how to teach them.

The teenagers we are trying to help are those who have failed to acquire the basic language skills of reading, writing, spelling and sometimes speech, despite normal intelligence, regular school attendance, and no discernible problems of sight, hearing, or emotional deprivation. In addition, they have been assessed as being dyslexic (or as having dyslexic-type problems) by qualified professionals administering standardised tests.

The comments in this book are all based on one-to-one

teaching. I am well aware that in many cases (and in many schools) group instruction may be inevitable, but progress is usually most rapid with individual teaching, and a teenager who has experienced many years of failure will feel more confident in a one-to-one situation. No two dyslexics have exactly the same difficulties, so individual lessons can concentrate immediately on each boy's particular problems.

This book is not in any way an exhaustive syllabus for the Secondary School child with learning difficulties. Its main aim is to show how the dyslexic adolescent can be guided and supported through all his struggles with language, so that he can eventually not only pass exams, but learn to cope with all the linguistic demands of life after school with realism and confidence.

The Problem

Helping a dyslexic of this age is very different from teaching a young dyslexic. The young child is not usually aware of the nature and extent of his handicap and he has no long history of failure. The older dyslexic has had a *daily* confrontation with failure, for perhaps 8 or 10 years. He may be good at art, or singing, he may play cricket well – but none of these skills is valued as highly in the world around him, even amongst his peers, as is literacy. Moreover, he cannot say to himself "I'm no good at that, so I'll give it up", as one can with music, or swimming, or art. In today's world, literacy is not an option, it's a necessity. So the teacher is likely to be faced with someone who has a poor opinion of himself, with (at the very least) feelings of inadequacy, if not frustration. He may well be very resistant to teaching, for if he hasn't so far managed to learn what comes so effortlessly to his friends, what's the point of trying any more? One of my duties during the last 10 years has been to administer a preliminary Dyslexia Test [1] to new boys entering school. One of the questions seeks to discover whether any other members of the family are similarly affected with literacy problems. Invariably, the answer from the boy concerned is "Yes, I've a brother, but *he's* bright".

Literacy is equated in his mind with high intelligence, so to be dyslexic is to be thick.

Again, with a young child, one doesn't assume he knows much – so one teaches him what a vowel is, what a sentence consists of, how to form his letters and join them up, how to work from left to right, up against the margin, using capital letters in the right places, and finishing off with a full stop. With an older dyslexic, one tends to assume that they know all this, and more – that they know what you mean when you talk about an adjective, or the past tense of a verb, or the need to write with clarity or logic. Clarity? Logic? Unknown words to the average dyslexic, but he won't admit it. He's got used to hearing words which he doesn't understand, and he's clever at agreeing and saying 'yes' to anyone in authority. It saves ridicule and unwelcome attention.

It must not therefore be assumed that anything is known. A lot will be – but checking up is quick and easy and avoids future muddle. The following dialogue is fairly typical.

Teacher:	You need to put -ed at the end of that word, because it's the past tense, isn't it?
Dyslexic:	Yes.
Teacher:	What do I mean by past tense?
Dyslexic:	Er – I don't know.
Teacher:	What's a verb?
Dyslexic:	Isn't it a name of something?

Two minutes' work on the lines of 'now, today, I play, but yesterday (in the past) I played' will soon sort out at least part of the problem (see Chapter 6 for naming parts of speech).

The teacher of the older dyslexic is dealing with a rich variety of pupils. Some have already had help, some haven't. Some are well-motivated, others don't want to know; some are very able, others are only average. Most will have picked up at least a smattering of reading and spelling, a few will have overcome their problems to a great extent. So the teacher's job is to check that the basics are known and understood (and if not, to start there and work forward systematically); to stitch up the holes and plug the gaps, and to have both general aims and specific individual goals.

Aims

The general aims should be:

a) fluent reading, for information and for pleasure. I used to put 'pleasure' first, before 'information'. But for some dyslexics, the dislike of reading has deep roots, and one can only hope that given time and tools, pleasure in reading will eventually grow.

b) logical spelling, at all times. The use of the word 'logical' is deliberate. When its meaning is made clear, it makes sense; to the older dyslexic, words can be frighteningly unpredictable in their spelling, a jumbled mass of arbitrary letters which he feels he cannot organise or categorise. 'Phonetically regular' would be more accurate than 'logical', but it sounds daunting and difficult, and impossible for him to achieve. In the Grand Canyon, where chipmunks and squirrels have learned not to fear the humans who give them tit-bits, there is a notice saying, "Feeding the squirrels is a no-no". To my mind, words like 'Phonetic' or 'rules' are no-no's too. Say 'logic' and 'principles' or 'patterns' instead, and remove the aura of association with school which equals failure.

c) a legible hand.

d) the ability to convey meaning accurately in speech and in writing.

Goals

The specific goals will vary for each individual according to his ability and degree of handicap, and they should, whenever possible, be discussed and agreed upon by teacher and pupil, thereby encouraging the pupil to feel involvement in, and responsibility for, his own progress and achievement. It goes without saying that the goals must be short-term and attainable. The severe dyslexic may be aiming for logic, whereas the milder case can aspire to some accuracy.

Is it too late to start teaching a dyslexic at 13 or even at 18? The answer must be no – sometimes it may be very difficult to alter long-standing and obdurate habits in reading and spelling and writing. But the increase in confidence, and the greater motivation and determination are not inconsiderable gains, and there is *always* progress towards that ultimate goal, literacy.

It will already be obvious that I refer exclusively to male dyslexics. It is strange that in our rich and complex language we have not yet adopted a useful neutral he/she amalgam. Until that happy day, I must apologise to female dyslexics (who are in the minority) and for reasons of ease and brevity, stick to 'he'.

Notes

1. Bangor Dyslexia Test: T.R. Miles (Learning Development Aids, Wisbech, Cambs.).

Chapter 2

Reading

"Reading maketh a full man"

(Bacon: Essays)

"Another damned, thick, square book!
Always scribble, scribble, scribble!"
(Duke of Gloucester 1743–1805)

Here then is the presenting problem: a boy of perhaps 14 or even older, who is struggling with an ever increasing load of classwork and homework, in many subjects; who is aware of already having 'failed' for 7 or 8 years, and is therefore either reluctant to try again, or fairly negative about the possibility of any improvement; he does not 'pick up' information in the way his non-dyslexic friends seem to, so he may be hazy about parts of speech, about what a tense is or what a verb does. He may read quite well (and he has perhaps even learned to read fast), but such reading may well be inaccurate and insufficiently grasped to give him the sense of it. He probably has a poor vocabulary, both for using (expressive) and understanding (receptive), and he tends to be a surface reader. By that I mean he cannot easily read between the lines, and he fails to understand figures of speech, such as metaphor or simile. In one short passage, which a dyslexic boy of 15 was reading, he was mystified by the expression 'the fringes of the field' ('a field doesn't have fringes, does it?') and later in the same passage, the phrase 'to drive it home' (of an argument) compounded his confusion. I asked him if he understood it – yes, it meant he was driving the car into the garage.

So reading is usually slow and tiring, and difficult to pick up again when it's not being done regularly. It is noticeable how much less well a boy will read after the holidays, or even after a weekend's break. Books are not always a pleasure – 'you'll not find a dyslexic who reads a book at bedtime for relaxation', I was told recently by an ex-pupil. A generalisation of course, and as such, untrue for the few, but most dyslexics would probably agree with him. Newspapers are scarcely read, except perhaps for the TV programmes and a little of the sports news – the layout, in columns which split up so many of the words, is difficult for maintaining meaning and fluency, and the language used is unfamiliar. It is felt by dyslexics that newspaper reading is time-wasting, not an efficient use of reading-time, and so the dyslexic misses out on important information and general knowledge. Helen Arkell[1] gives an excellent account of reading a Sunday newspaper: 'it may not be the relaxing occupation that it might appear. At first glance some headline will catch his eye, and he may read on. A drink of coffee will take his eye from the page, and when he looks back exactly the same headline will catch his eye, but until he actually *reads* it again, he will not be aware of having seen it before.' That is, at the very least, an irritation. A dyslexic becomes heavily dependent on auditory sources of information – radio, TV or tapes – and is unable and unwilling to join in conversations about external matters which he fears will show up his ignorance and make him feel inferior.

Then there is the constant problem of mis-reading. If you omit the word 'not' in reading the following message, 'he will not be able to take you driving on Sunday', exactly the opposite meaning is achieved to the one intended. And at a more advanced stage, if you are a chemist and read cyclohex*a*ne instead of cyclohex*e*ne, you may have a costly and dangerous accident on your hands.

Interest and Relevance

How then to help with reading. Interest and relevance are crucial at this Secondary stage. It may give us as teachers a feeling of satisfaction if we can persuade our pupils to read a good book (and indeed it frequently gives them great satisfaction too). But for many reluctant and incompetent readers, it is far more important to catch their unwilling attention by helping them to read what they want to know – be it a technical journal, the sports news, a difficult chapter in a text-book, or even a piece of simple writing about themselves. Some years ago, I taught a tough lad of 15 who not only *couldn't* read, no way was he ever going to do anything so wet and sissy, much more profit in mugging old ladies or pinching things in Woolworths. He would not sit up to the desk and flatly refused to even open a book. The next time he came I handed him a letter, with his name on the envelope. Not many people can resist a letter, and luckily nor could he. Inside I had written a few brief and extremely simple sentences about him – and none too polite either. From then on, I had his interest and he learned to read. His social behaviour may not have improved, but at least I felt he could amuse himself with books if he ended up in prison.

For reading to make progress, it is necessary to know all the vowel sounds and vowel digraphs, for safe recall and recognition. Most consonants will already be known, but some unusual consonant combinations may need pointing out – 'ch' as in architecture and 'ph'. It is useful to link these sounds with well-known words e.g. *sch*ool and *ph*one, so the pupil becomes used to thinking of ch as not only a *ch*ip sound, but possibly a *sch*ool sound. C and g need pointing out too, though learning is always best if the boy himself discovers the pattern underlying soft and hard c and g. So it may help to make 2 short lists:

cat	gas
cent	gents
city	gin
cot	got
cut	gun
cycle	gym

C's first. What do these 6 words have in common? All begin with

c. Right. Look at the vowel after it – now put the 6 words into 2 groups, according to the sound made by the c. By this time they have:

k	cat
s	cent
s	city
k	cot
k	cut
s	cycle

Then repeat the exercise with the 'g' words.

g	gas
j	gents
j	gin
g	got
g	gun
j	gym

Then compare the 2 lists. By this time the dyslexic can deduce for himself that usually c and g are soft before e, i and y. (Always stress 'usually'; unfortunately very common and well-known words such as 'girl' tend to spoil the pattern.)

Vowel Digraphs

The vowel digraphs which must be known for successful reading (as well as, of course, spelling) are:

a – e	(same)	e – e	(Pete)	i – e	(pipe)
ai	(rain)	ee	(see)	ie	(pie)
ay	(day)	ea	(sea)	igh	(light)
		ie	(field)		
		ei	(ceiling)		

o – e	(rope)	u – e	(tube)
oe	(toe)	ue	(glue)
oa	(boat)	ew	(new)
ow	(snow)		

Also: ou (out)   oo (moon)   oi (boil)   au (cause)
       ow (how)   oy (boy)   aw (saw)

I realise there are others (e.g. 'ui' as in fruit), but one needs to beware of over-loading the memory for the sake of a few words, which can often be recognised in context. 'igh' is also a slight problem to the purist, as it is of course not a vowel digraph. But the words using it are so common that frequency justifies its inclusion in the list.

Long and Short Vowels

A more serious problem arises with the concept of 'long' and 'short' vowels. I find that some dyslexics have trouble with these 2 words, which are meaningless for them in the context of vowel sounds. ā and ă are neither long nor short, they're sounds of letters. It's as if one were asking whether an apple is rich or poor. An apple is a fruit. Rich and poor are not appropriate words to use. I find it more helpful to talk in terms of 'a' saying its name in certain positions and saying ă in others.

Assuming that most consonant blends and vowel digraphs can be recognised, it is also a help to be familiar with the common prefixes and suffixes, such as de-, re-, se-, per-, pre-, pro-, and -tion, -ly, -ment, -ance/ence, -able, -ible. This means that 'depend' will be read as de-pend, rather than as dep-end, and the dyslexic can then teach himself to block off the familiar bits at the beginning and ending of a word, and only has to sort out what's left in the middle:

con-struc-tion
pre-vent-able

Strategies

So now (in theory) the pupil knows all his letter sounds, vowel combinations, and a fistful of prefixes and suffixes (and don't forget to explain carefully the meaning of the words 'prefix' and 'suffix', and of every linguistic term used, as it crops up). But he still can't read very well. A variety of strategies can be adopted.

a)   if he's starting to read a new book, or a new chapter, or even a pamphlet or instruction kit – read the first paragraph *to* him (even, in the case of a book, the first chapter or a good part of it). This plugs him in to the right context, he knows what sort of language he has to deal with, whether it's straightforward or complex, funny or serious, factual or imaginative. It will engage his interest, and lead him into friendly territory, rather than into the daunting unknown.

b)   read alternately with him. This makes sense if it's a play or dialogue, but it also serves several useful purposes in straight reading, in that he can pick up from you the importance of putting expression into the voice; he can manage to cope with a short, clearly defined section, whereas an unending page of words is like heaven – so impossible to reach that one might as well not even set out on the path to it.

c)   provide the difficult words for him. If he's managing to keep going fairly fluently and has a good grasp of what's going on, to have to stop and puzzle out a new and complex word is a sure recipe for reinforcing his conviction that reading will never be easy or fun.

d)   read to him again, but this time (to make sure he's following) play verbal musical chairs; when you stop in mid-sentence, he has to read the next word or phrase. It's astonishing how often words which are normally stumbling blocks can be readily produced in this way. It is also noticeable that words in isolation (as in 'Phonic Rummy'[2]) can frequently be read quickly and easily, whereas the same words grouped together in a sentence can cause stumbling and hesitation. I think the answer lies in the amount of material to be read. Just as we cannot eat a whole sausage in one go, but can easily manage and enjoy it if it's cut up into bits, so a dyslexic can manage bite-size words or phrases, but gags at endless lines of script. It helps if one can make him aware of punctuation – to notice actively the full stops and commas, and not to set out on reading a sentence without seeing where the next halt is. The task then becomes manageable – he's not reading unending lines of words, but is instead going from halt to halt as it were. Incidentally, I often wish punctuation were more visible – full stops, commas, and even question and exclamation marks are easily overlooked by the dyslexic, and one sometimes longs for musical bar lines or their linguistic equivalent.

e)   clue-hunting. Make reading more fun (even text-books) by learning to look for clues. Pictures, diagrams and sketches, of course, but titles, chapter headings, capital letters and proper names can all give some idea of what to expect, before actually starting to read.

f)   if the dyslexic is to maintain any sort of fluency or interest in reading, he has to make guesses occasionally, and it is both unrealistic and cruel to expect him to do otherwise. But it is perfectly possible to encourage *sensible* guessing, in the context of what he's reading. So in the sentence 'he scratched his head and looked perplexed', 'puzzled' would have to be an acceptable alternative to 'perplexed', but 'prefixed' would not.

Continuity in reading can also be promoted by recognising that the important part of a *long* word is usually the beginning of it, but the converse is true for a short word. So if one can read *per* in 'perspective' accurately, one is more likely to read the word which relates to scale, than the one which means 'future' (*pro*spective). But obviously in 'had' or 'they', the last letter is important if one is not to confuse 'had' with 'has' and 'they' with 'them'.

Words are Fun

In encouraging reading, I think it is important to stress that it can be pleasurable, that words can be played with. Poor reading is partially due to lack of reading which in itself is due to fear. If it can be shown that you can manipulate words, turn them around to make other words, invent brand-new words, then fear of reading can be minimised. Words should be seen to be tools which people use. Anagrams, palindromes, nonsense words (as in Lear or Lewis Carroll), simple crosswords, can be used to get this point across. 'Radar' and 'level' are more acceptable as palindromes (and more easily remembered for spelling) and palindromic phrases such as 'able was I ere I saw Elba' or 'a man, a plan, a canal, Panama' can be a revelation to the word-bound dyslexic.

Ensuring Reading

To ensure that a dyslexic is reading when he's not actually being taught can be tricky. One 45-minute lesson a week (or occasionally 2 if one's lucky) is not enough to keep reading going, so the pupil has to be sent away to read. The conscientious one *will* read, dutifully, but very often without understanding or great interest. The average boy will flip through a page or two, or skim, and hope to goodness he won't be asked awkward questions about it, or that somebody will tell him the gist of it. To guard against both these ploys, there are two remedies. One is to ask him to give you a brief oral or written account of what he's been reading, but the better one in my own experience, is this: I send him away to read a few pages, and he then prepares 4 or 5 very obscure questions based on what he's read (such as 'what time did X join his ship?' 'Was it raining?'). When he comes for his lesson the following week, he allows me 90 seconds to skim through the same pages and pick up as much detail as I can. He then puts the questions to me. Inevitably I fail on at least half of them. This makes him feel good, and moreover he has thoroughly read and understood the relevant passage.

There are of course many dyslexics in this age group who are good and eager readers. It is still important though to check that they are also, when required, accurate readers. Answering some questions well depends as much on reading them carefully as on writing down the answers. A misunderstood question wins no marks, and misunderstanding can arise from misreading.

What to Read?

For the poor reader, there are now several series of abridged books. Some offer the classics, others modern best sellers such as 'Jaws', Ian Fleming's James Bond books, Alastair Maclean. These are good in that the dyslexic can feel he is not missing out on what his friends are reading, but inevitably the style of the original book is lost, and the actions are so compressed as to make the plot rather dense. Being short, they can be read from start to finish in a reasonable time, which does give a feeling of achievement. Humorous books are sometimes suitable, though on the whole passages need to be hand-picked by the teacher. Gerald Durrell's books are good for this, as are David Nobbs' two books about Reginald Perrin, and Clive James has been known to turn a reluctant reader into an enthusiast. Adrian Mole's gloomy adventures[3] are popular too. Narrative poetry can also serve – the strong rhythm and the repetitive devices are useful props, and the rhyming pattern helps in anticipating the words. 'The Ancient Mariner' is an example. For the reluctant reader, who is 'bored with books', short stories may engage his interest. There are good selections available nowadays of short stories about science fiction or space fantasies. There is also an excellent series of fantastic adventure books which require reader participation; the reader has to make choices and use dice, and depending on his choice, will be sent scurrying around the book having various adventures.[4]

Books which are based on popular TV series or programmes such as Grange Hill or the Vet Books, can stimulate a sluggish book-appetite, and so can tapes; there are on the market now many excellent readings on tape of all sorts of books from

Shakespeare to recent best sellers. Many of the set-books required by the examination boards can be found on tape now and they can be a very useful aid to reading.

Interest must, however, be engaged –and very often only reading seen to be relevant will do that. This is when one has to read journals on farming, magazines on BMX-ing, instructions for assembling a kit, a chapter on the refraction of light, or the small print on a driving licence application form. One must, as a teacher, accept that for some dyslexics, reading will never be a pleasure, but it can nevertheless become a useful and usable tool.

Notes

1. Dyslexia: Introduction – A Dyslexic's Eye View by Helen Arkell (The Helen Arkell Dyslexia Centre, 14 Crandace Road, London, 1975).
2. Phonic Rummy: (12 Packs of Cards) 1973 (Kenworthy Educational Service Inc., Buffalo, N.Y.) Obtainable from Better Books, 15A Chelsea Road, Lower Weston, Bath.
3. See Book List, p. 96.
4. See Book List, p. 96.

Chapter 3

Spelling

"Do you spell it with a 'V' or a 'W'?" enquired the judge.
"That depends upon the taste and fancy of the speller,
my Lord" replied Sam

(Dickens: Pickwick Papers)

It is when dealing with spelling that the differences between young dyslexics and teenage dyslexics become most marked. With a young child the slate is almost clean; one can start at the very beginning and work slowly and systematically in a structured way through the English spelling system. In the case of the older dyslexic, many spelling patterns and grammatical rules have already been absorbed. He may not know how to lengthen the vowel sounds, but he recognises the suffix 'tion' and can use it. He may know how to spell 'daughter', but 'caught' is a puzzle. To him, spelling is very probably a confusing, if not hopeless, rag-bag which he despairs of ever sorting out, and yet which is accorded great importance by all around him. Scragg[1] wrote 'Public censure of the bad speller has a long history . . . whereas in the 18th century such signs of ignorance (i.e. bad spelling) attracted only ridicule, in the 19th, as the modern emphasis on qualification by examination came into being, the bad speller might find his livelihood threatened by his disability. Our educational system lays considerable emphasis on the teaching of correct spelling, and the continuing popularity of spelling bees, of spelling questions in general knowledge tests, shows that the ability to memorise the traditional spelling is widely believed to be a mark of full education. Society condemns those who cannot spell.'

16

Lord Chesterfield in 1750 rebuked his son for a mis-spelling and quoted the case of a 'man of quality who never recovered from the ignominy of spelling 'wholesome' without the w.' We are not much more tolerant today – bad spelling is still thought to be a sign of ignorance or stupidity. And yet – Shakespeare himself spelled his own name in at least 6 different ways, and Charles Darwin consistently mis-spelt 'yacht' and 'board' (yatch/broad).

It is useful I think at this stage to try and sort out the rag-bag and pull out the important bits. Like patchwork, once you've decided where the main pieces are to go, the others will sort themselves out around them to form a pleasing and ordered pattern. The important 'bits' in spelling at this later stage are, I think, vowel sounds, doubling, the root word and Law of Probabilities, and I will deal with these in turn. I do not intend to go in any detail into how to teach spelling – there are many, many books on the market which do just that better than I ever could. The following are tips and suggestions which I have found *do* work.

It should be made clear from the outset that accuracy cannot always be achieved. To expect perfection is unrealistic and unkind. However, *logic* in spelling, always, is an attainable goal and moreover, it makes written communication possible and successful. The aim of writing is not correct spelling, it is to communicate messages, thoughts or ideas, as meaningfully as possible.

Vowels

It is important to check first of all that the early stages of spelling are safe; that the various vowel sounds are known, that doubling is understood, and that simple prefixes and suffixes are recognised. Usually none of these *are* safe – but instead of tackling one vowel digraph at a time ('ee', say) as with the younger child, one groups together all the various ways of spelling the long 'e' sound, in order of frequency. At this stage ee (see) and ea (sea) will be well-known, and e-e (these) is rare, so ie (field) and ei after s or c (ceiling) are the ones to concentrate on. The aim is to familiarise the pupil with all the possible spellings, so that a sensible choice can be made in the case of an unknown word. 'Interfere' may come out as 'interfear', but it should not be 'interfeir'.

A helpful way to remember the main possibilities is to work out mnemonic sentences. They work best if the dyslexic himself has devised them, but I have found that the following are short enough to be reliably recalled on demand:

For a:	Say the name of the train
For e:	Pete has a cheap green field
For i:	My nine bright ties
For o:	Joe hopes to go to the Boat Show
For u:	a new tube of glue

Similar mnemonics could be made up for other vowel digraphs (and a different 'i' might be needed for a girl!).

The vowel digraphs au/aw (cause/lawn) are usually very difficult to remember, as the obvious choice for that sound is 'or'. It is useful to point out that the sound needed is in 'saw', (which is happily nearly always known by now and only rarely confused with 'was') and then to ask what other letter in the alphabet is like 'w'? You may get a blank look at this stage, but if you say 'double u' very slowly and deliberately, light dawns. Then ask whether you can spell 'saw' with an 'au'? No, because 'u' is not usually at the end of an English word. So where could you put 'au'? In the middle of a word, or at the beginning (August). Thereafter, it is safe to say that, fraud and haunt for instance are 'saw' words. 'Aw' is not possible in that position, so it must be 'au' – usually. One immediately thinks of 'lawn' or 'awl', but they are special cases and life is too short and spelling too complex to worry about them. (In any case, by a merciful dispensation of providence I have found that 'lawn' is nearly always known.)

It is worth spending quite a lot of thought and time on 'e'. It is such an extraordinarily multi-purpose tool (rather like a scout's penknife) and the danger is that some dyslexics get the feeling they should pop it in whenever and wherever something looks wrong. So it needs tidying up and categorising. Its main functions are:

a) to lengthen a short vowel sound (cap, cape)
b) to soften a 'c' or a 'g' (ice, cage)
c) to prevent a 'plural' effect (please, horse)
    Without the 'e', the words above would look as if they were the plural forms of 'plea' and 'hor'. I do not claim that this is a historically justified rationale – but it is a rationale that works. Dyslexics tend to write hous and choos, and since the 'e' doesn't seem to be needed for any other reason, it could well be that it's there because an 's' at the end of a word *looks* like a plural. This is readily appreciated by dyslexics, by analogy with cat (one cat) and cats (more than one).

d) to allow a word to end in a 'z' or 'v' sound:
    freez (single syllable words usually have zz, as in 'fuzz'
    liv
e) 'e' is also the vowel most commonly used to represent the indeterminate noise we make when we open our mouths, drop our jaws, and let a sound out (the 'schwa' sound) – as in mother, level, generate, sentence.

The 'e' serves few other useful functions, so it is not needed (and is therefore wrong) in, for example, sorte and kinde.

Doubling

This concept (of doubling the consonant following a short vowel) causes more problems, and is more susceptible to misuse, than any other principle of spelling at the secondary stage, in my experience. Nearly all dyslexics have *heard* of it, and have the fuzziest notions of what it means and how it works. But the net effect is that they *don't* apply it, and don't know how to, except sometimes in known words such as 'better' or 'butter'.

I have already said that the idea of 'long' and 'short' vowels is a difficult one to grasp. And yet it is fundamental to the understanding of doubling, so how to get around the problem? In North Wales, we are surrounded by the ruins of the mediaeval castles built by Edward I, and I have found they provide a splendid and easily-grasped analogy for doubling. In simplified form, each castle consists of a keep, surrounded by two walls. Between the two walls is a moat or ditch. The invader from outside could fairly easily breach *one* wall, but he would then find himself either in the moat, or being drenched in boiling oil. So the keep is safe and unattacked. If however the keep were surrounded by only *one* wall, the hypothetical invader could get through and capture it.

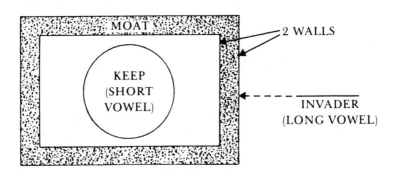

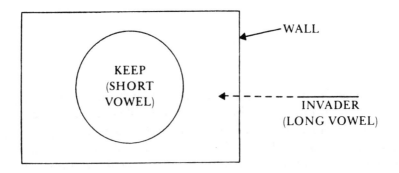

Back now to doubling. The keep is the weak (short) vowel, which needs protecting from the invader (the following vowel); if the invader has only one wall (or consonant) to get through, the weak vowel will be attacked and changed,

as in: d*in* + er – diner

To prevent such a change, there must be a double wall (2 consonants)

as in: dinn + er –di*nn*er

The analogy seems childish, but it works. Having explained it once, it is then only necessary to say 'protect your weak vowel' or 'do you need a double wall?' as the situation arises. Mistakes still occur, of course, but the principle is understood.

The Root Word

A lot of the spelling mistakes made by older dyslexics are of the 'squeeze-box' variety – that is, the word has been compressed so that vital letters are omitted and the sense may be lost. 'Arst' and 'ented' are two such. It helps to know about the 'rootword', and a two minute session with the daily paper, pulling out 10 words and finding the root of each, makes the point. But it does need constant nagging – in the full flow of composition it's all too easy to write 'he jumpt out of bed'.

What's the root of 'arst'? Ask. And so what do you need to add? -ed. So the spelling should be 'asked'. 'Slipped' looks splendid – doubling correct too. But in this sentence:

'the boy was slipped when he climbed in the window'

it's not immediately obvious that the word actually intended was 'slipp*ered*'.

The root word is needed as well when it's a question of terminal 'y' changing to 'i'. 'Happly he walked in the wood' is not a quaint way of saying perhaps. What is the root word? Happy. Adding ? ly. So change the 'y' of happy to 'i', and add 'ly'. Happily.

The logs burnt *redly*? No, in fact the logs burnt *readily*.

To find the root is important too when spelling long, multi-syllabic words. Not so much because the whole word may be squeezed, but because the root of it is the first building block on which prefixes and suffixes have to be hooked, and for dyslexics some bricks tend to get lost unless each link is carefully made.

So, 'importantly' may come out as 'importly' unless 'port' is pulled out, as the root, 'im' hooked on the front, and 'ant', then 'ly' at the back.

What has happened is that the 't' of 'import' was taken to be the final 't'. If you say importantly fast enough, you can see that this could be so.

'Finely' is another example. Perfectly good word, too. But not in the context of 'Finely we won the match'.

Laws of Probabilities

A grand title for a simple idea. We must never lose sight of the fact that our ultimate aim is to provide our dyslexics with adequate, if rough and ready, tools to cope with spelling on their own. We are not there to help when they're sitting O-levels, or CSE's. Nor are we around when they've left school and are writing letters to prospective employers, or girl friends, or filling in forms. In Neurogenic Communicative Disorders,[2] the author is talking about patients with brain damage affecting speech – but the point he makes is relevant to teaching dyslexics too:

> . . . regardless of the method or what it does for the (patient) while he is under the (clinician's) guiding, urging hand, if it leaves (the patient) impotent outside the clinic, it is only manipulation.

So I think we have to teach *probabilities*, the most likely spelling for a new word or a forgotten one. This is a logical approach, which will ensure perhaps 75% success or even higher.

a)   The 'ur' sound is a case in point. There are 5 different ways in English of spelling it – er, ir, ur, or and ear. 'Or' only ever comes after a w if it is to make the 'ur' sound (w*or*ld), so we can forget that one. Er/ir/ur are the most common ways of spelling it, and just because of that, most simple words in each group are known by this time (term, serve, her; sir, first, bird; turn, Thursday, purse, nurse). This leaves the 'ear' group of words, only about half a dozen of them in regular usage. So *those* are the ones it's important to know thoroughly. They are:

earn, learn, heard, search, pearl.

Of course there are others, such as earl, hearse. But they are rare enough to leave off the memory load. So, a new word with the 'ur' sound, e.g. turpentine? It won't be 'or' (since there is no 'w' in front of it). It won't be 'ear' (because they're known). So it must be er/ir or ur. At this stage, if it is important, try the look of it:

*ter*pentine
*tir*pentine
*tur*pentine

and try analogy. Turn? Yes. So reasoned elimination leads to turpentine.

b)   Another example. What one could call the 'ul' sound – spelt le, al, el (tab*le*, anim*al*, lev*el*). A little research in a rhyming dictionary shows that 'le' is far and away the most common ending, followed by 'al', with 'el' trailing well behind. But some 'el' words are important (level, funnel, rebel, parcel, gravel) – so a short list of these is called for, and as for the rest: if in doubt, put 'le'.

c)   The 'sh' sound. A nasty and difficult sound when it appears in the middle of a word, spelt variously -ti, -ci, or -si (though

-si usually makes a 'zh' sound, as in vi*si*on). But this too can be mastered, if logic and the law of probabilities are applied to it.

The obvious way to spell any word with the 'sh' sound, is by using sh –

*sh*ip
di*sh*

and that is how most dyslexics will attempt to spell, say, 'speshal'. But in the middle of words, the 'sh' sound is almost never spelt 'sh'. (There are 5 fairly common words which do use 'sh' in the middle of a word – wor*sh*ip, bi*sh*op, cu*sh*ion, fa*sh*ion, mar*sh*al.) There are then the 3 possible ways -ti, -ci and -si, but which to choose? Again the rhyming dictionary gives the answer. 'ti' is 9 times more common as a spelling for words with the 'sh' sound in the middle of them, than ci or si. So again, needed or common words with 'ci' need to be known (special, suspicious, racial); the 'zh' sound needs to be taught as being spelt with si or su (television; pleasure). And for all the rest – if you put 'ti' you'll be right nine times out of ten.

In showing a dyslexic how to apply laws of probability, he is learning how to generalise. He learns to deduce, to make reasoned guesses, and he is not having to rely on his dodgy memory.

Accurate Spelling

All this may sound very haphazard and loose. Are we never to expect accurate spelling, or demand it? Yes, indeed we are, in two very important groups of words.

(1)   Proper nouns and technical terms. Authors and names of books have to be exactly spelt in English exams. Place names, mountains, and rivers in Geography. Battles and

generals and rulers in History. In the Sciences, commonly used words like protein, amoeba, chemicals, hydrogen, pressure – these have to be known.

(2)   Small, tricky words in everyday use: does and goes, their, through, every; any and many; would, could and should. And so on. It is a curious fact that most people who can accept a misspelling in a word like apearance or appearence, will see red when they meet 'meny' or 'coud'. (A full list of such words, necessary for everyday writing, can be found in my 'Check-List for Dyslexics'.[3])

More Help for Spelling

I have already mentioned mnemonics as possible learning-aids. There are many others.

a)   Use of clues and tips.
       Which right is right for righting a letter? You *write* on wh*ite* paper
       which beach is which? the b*ea*ch by the *sea*
                             the b*ee*ch tr*ee*
       *bir*ds ch*ir*p
       the *cat ca*ught a mouse ('caught' is frequently misspelt 'cought')
       p*ie*ce of p*ie*; p*ea*ce *a*nd w*a*r
       th*ei*r (always a difficult one). It belongs to *they*, so change the y to i, and add r
       O my s*o*n.
       The clues and tips will tend to be personal and individual to each dyslexic, and more safely remembered if he's thought of them himself.

b)   Mispronunciations. Some words are so awkward and phonetically irregular, that they can only be remembered by pronouncing them wrongly (or differently)
       talk (talc)
       friend (fri-end)
       some (so me)

was (wăs, americanised)
genuine (genuĭne, americanised)

c)   Association. A pupil of mine some years ago could never remember how to spell 'friend' (even by the above method). Eventually, we associated it with Friday – you meet your *fri*end on a *Fri*day. This worked excellently even though for several months thereafter she had to actually write down Friday first then cross it out, whenever she needed to write 'friend'!

d)   Family groups.

here	could	though
*t*here	would	th*r*ough
*w*here	should	though*t*

are examples of families. There are many more.

e)   Nonsense words. These can be very helpful, as the dyslexic has to really *think* how to spell, he cannot rely on his faulty memory.

f)   A personal dictionary. This can be a simple notebook, but better is a tabulated address book where the letters of the alphabet run down the right hand side of the book. In it the dyslexic can put all the words which *he* needs to be able to spell, or which have a tricky bit which could catch him unawares, such as mor*t*gage, parli*a*ment, pe*o*ple. If the rogue letter is underlined or highlighted, it will catch his attention whenever he turns to that page. Incidentally, it may be very cheering to point out that 90% of all writing uses only 1,000 words!

g)   Subject vocabularies. I have already said that accuracy in spelling *is* necessary in the case of technical terms, proper names etc. This may sound very demanding, but in fact the advanced spelling required for subject vocabularies is usually comparatively easy. This is because such words are often more phonetically regular, and can be grouped into categories, such as all words ending in -ology, or -itis; or beginning with bio- or anti-.

The subject vocabulary can be compiled from two

sources: 1) the subject teacher may be willing to supply a list of essential words and 2) old exam papers in the subject can be acquired; these usually contain a comprehensive specialist vocabulary which can be copied on to file cards, in logical or alphabetical groupings, and either pinned up on the bedroom or study wall, or slipped into a plastic wallet or diary – anywhere in fact where they are available and visible.

h) Theme cards. Using file cards again, lists of words can be compiled for various themes. Numbers, perhaps, on one (very useful for writing cheques). Months of the year, days of the week and seasons on another. Words used in letter-writing on a third – sincerely, truly, faithfully, received, Mr and Mrs; the pupil's own name and address written in block capitals – dyslexics often have greatly difficulty in writing consistently in capitals. I have known several who have to write out their address in lower case letters first, then transcribe it into capitals; this is not only laborious, but potentially embarrassing if it has to be done in public.

i) Word-Games can be used to help spelling. Simple Scrabble and easy crosswords are good, in that each word depends on another and, in the case of crosswords, it has to be correctly spelt, or it won't fit. Anagrams can be pressed into service too (after all, many dyslexic spelling mistakes *are* anagrams), and the boy who writes 'aronud' for 'around' will usually be able to sort himself out if you place the letters of the word in a circle and ask him to spell it:

The popular spelling game 'Hangman' can be well adapted for use at different stages of difficulty, or to stress a particular pattern; it also promotes familiarity with the letters which frequently go together.

Finally, I hope I have made it clear that spelling requires some basic knowledge, a lot of informed deduction and, always, a logical approach. And, in the last resort, a dash of bluff. Does that long multisyllabic word end in -able or -ible? Is it -ance or -ence? There is no certain way of knowing (without consulting a dictionary), so 'experience' is written with a slightly blurred penultimate 'e' (or 'a'). 'Audible' has a similarly blurred 'i' (or 'a'). This is not cheating. Writing is communication – and communication is successful if the reader sees what he expects to see, and understands the meaning which the writer intends to convey.

Notes

1. 'A History of English Spelling', D.G. Scragg (Manchester University Press, 1974).
2. 'Clinical Management of Communicative Disorders' ed. by Donnell F. Johns PhD (Little, Brown & Co., Boston, 1978).
3. 'Spelling Check-Lists: Dictionary for Dyslexics' E.G. Stirling (St David's College, Llandudno, Gwynedd, 1984).

Chapter 4

Punctuation

The use of punctuation is very difficult to teach. The dyslexic pupil seems to have no natural feel for it, and is quite capable of going on for lines on end without any full stops or commas. When he is made aware of the need for a pause he may put it in at arbitrary intervals or in the wrong place –

I went to bed. So that I would be fresh in the morning I got up early and had a swim.

A boy I once taught had learned that writing needed punctuating. He was a good and fluent writer and presented me one day with a 3-page essay. No punctuation to speak of. When I tackled him, he looked pained, 'but look, I've put 3 full stops on each page!'

It helps to decide which are the priorities. Full stops, capital letters at the beginning of a new sentence. Commas, quite often. Question marks occasionally. Colons, semi-colons, exclamation marks are icing on the cake and can be dispensed with. I'm almost tempted to say that apostrophes can too; I find that so many people (not only dyslexics) misuse apostrophes, and scatter them wholesale like currants in a bun, in plurals (cat's and dog's), or in the wrong part of an abbreviated word (hav'nt, is'nt), that on the whole it is probably safer to tell a dyslexic *not* to use them unless they're absolutely certain where to. The sentence immediately preceding this one would be just as clear (and more elegant, one might justifiably say) had I put 'they are' instead of 'they're'.

Speech marks are a great hazard, and if one thinks about it,

29

almost never necessary in everyday writing. Even dialogue is now rarely written with speech marks – and almost the only users are novelists who need to convey speech between more than two people, and reporters quoting comments from members of the public.

An English exam (O-level or CSE) not infrequently asks for a dialogue between, say, a teenage boy and his mother, who complains of his staying out late each evening. Speech marks can certainly be dispensed with in such a case, and the technique to use is simply to name the speaker at the beginning of each line of dialogue, e.g.

Tom:
Mother:
Jo:

The reason for trying to avoid speech marks is that dyslexics get hopelessly confused about where and when to put them, and can sometimes not differentiate between direct speech and reported speech.

'I said I would go' may come out as: I said 'I would go' and a longer sentence, such as:

'We must go to London', said Fred, 'we have to visit some friends' is likely to be written 'We must go to London said Fred, we have to visit some friends'.

Examples of writing without punctuation help to make it clear that some sort of sign is needed to convey meaning accurately. A simple example from an impeccable source is:

'And they found Mary and Joseph and the Babe lying in a manger'; and the following is not only an excellent object-lesson, but fun too:

Mary where Jane had had had had had had had had had had had the teacher's approval (for those totally confused, put in a comma after Mary, the 3rd had, and a full stop after the 7th had).

Also, try to make the pupil become aware of where the voice pauses, where a breath can be taken, where the voice lifts. At all such halts along the line, a comma, full stop or question-mark can probably be inserted.

But the only true essentials in punctuations are the full stop, the capital letter, and occasionally a comma. Restricting, perhaps – but a large body of good writing can be achieved with such bare necessities. The following quotations make the point:

(1) The autumn when he went to Mill Hill School saw considerable changes in our home life. Jonathan had gone to university in 1969 and now Mark also went off to college. For most of the year David was virtually an only child. (From 'A Message from the Falklands' by David Tinker West, RN, Penguin 1983.)

(2) Slowly his head and arms came down. He no longer grinned. He took a step forward and turned. Then he began to run down river, not fast, but keeping as near to the water as he could. ('The Inheritors' by William Golding.)

Chapter 5

Handwriting

'How can you contrive to write so even?'
(Jane Austen: Pride and Prejudice)

When considering handwriting, I think we must try to be clear in our minds about what handwriting looks like, and what it is for. If I go to buy a teapot, my main requirement must be that it pours well and fluently, without dripping, and that I can hold it comfortably without burning my hand. If I choose one on looks alone, I may find when I get it home that it doesn't work very well. The ideal of course is to combine design and function. A knife is no good to me, however aesthetically pleasing, if it's so top heavy that it falls off the plate whenever I clear the dishes.

So, in handwriting, the first requirement must be legibility. That is its function: to communicate ideas, thoughts, information to the reader. Robert Bridges held that 'true legibility consists in the certainty of deciphering'.

I think we make unfair demands on handwriting. We expect to read it with the ease of a printed text. Since everybody's handwriting is unique, and different from everyone else's, it is surely almost a miracle that we can read it at all. But we demand not only legibility – we like it to look good too, to satisfy certain arbitrary standards of neatness or beauty. We do not expect a hammer to be a work of art, to hang on a wall for our friends to admire, and nor should we expect handwriting to do more than get the message over. Modern calligraphers have got it right, I think – calligraphy is an art form, not primarily a method of communicating words and meanings.

A dyslexic of 13 or 14 comes to us with many problems, and handwriting may be one of them. His writing may alter in slant, it may be messy and crabby, and wander over the page. He may form his letters curiously, or have trouble keeping his words on the line, or he may make his writing too big or too small – and all these may affect legibility, and moreover, influence his reader's perception of the *content* of his writing. So, for the dyslexic, it is important for him to present work which is as pleasing as possible. His spelling will already handicap him, so he must avoid compounding the problem by writing which is messy or annoying.

I feel very strongly about dyslexics and handwriting, for we demand of them a standard which very few of us adhere to ourselves. Many professional people, who spend a large part of their lives using pen or pencil, have the most appalling hand – the GP writing his prescriptions is well-known. I am often shown classwork or homework done by a dyslexic boy which has been marked and commented upon by his teacher. Can he read the comments? No, not really. In one case, the boy concerned was anxious to know how he'd done, and had managed with some difficulty to decipher most of the critique. The final remark floored him though, so he brought it to me. It was, 'what diabolical handwriting, X, you really should be more careful'.

Priorities

Again, as with punctuation, it's all a question of priorities. What are the essentials we have to insist on, and what can we ignore? We are dealing with adolescents, who by this time already have a well-established style of their own, however awful, so we have to make do and mend, rather than go back to square one and start from scratch. And the pupil has to see the point of improving his writing – his attitude is sometimes 'too bad if he can't read it', but he'll change his tune when he sees he can't read it himself a week later, or when he's trying to revise for an exam.

Established letter formation we have to accept on the whole, except where a faulty letter leads to ambiguity. This often arises in the case of 'o' which degenerates into 'a', or vice versa, e.g. 'wos' instead of 'was', 'u' which ends at the top (v) before joining the next letter, or 'w' which comes *down* before joining. Such errors hinder legibility, and only practice will eradicate them, though the message gets over clearly if the teacher writes words or sentences with the offending letters malformed and asks the dyslexic to read them.

e.g. 'Whot doy is holf-term?'

The most confusing letters which must be clearly written are w, u, v, m and n. A word such as 'woman' or 'wander' or 'worm' can easily be written so as to be completely unreadable.

A malformed 'e', on the other hand (written from the bottom up) may *look* awkward, to the observer, but may be so normal to the writer, and part of his style, that it would be unwise to tamper with it.

It is surprising to find that some pupils have really no clear idea of where on the line they should place letters. This particularly applies to letters which sit on the line with their tails hanging below (though 'g' is not often the culprit). This results in words like PeoPle or Joint or Your. Such errors are thought to be capitals in the wrong place (and sometimes they are), but they can also be misplaced lower-case ones and a little work is needed therefore on this aspect.

A consistent slope should be encouraged – not for artistic reasons but because the reader has otherwise to shift his viewpoint to accommodate it, which is annoying. Again, a written example from the teacher will make the point. Writing in to the margin is something everyone can and must learn to do, as it greatly improves the appearance of a piece of writing. Writing which wanders erratically over towards the right hand side of the page looks childish – a strong argument!

Writing which is too small is quite hard to remedy – though curiously I have found that when confidence in spelling improves, so does the size of the letters. It's as if the dyslexic thinks that if he makes the writing small enough, spelling mistakes won't be spotted. Example again, may be all that is needed – a miniscule piece of one's own writing is extraordinarily hard for a dyslexic to read.

A more difficult point to get over, is when writing is too big. The solution here is to point out how very hard it is to identify a picture, or an advertisement on a hoarding, if one is too close to it. Or to say what an object is if one is only shown a small, highly-magnified part of it (a device used successfully in the TV quiz game 'Ask the Family').

It can also be pointed out that it is much harder to read a passage
fluently when
there are only
two or three
words on a line
as in newspaper
columns
than if one can have a good run at a sizeable chunk of writing.

Messiness can be cleaned up nowadays with splendid ink-erasers. But the dyslexic should be urged to put one simple line through a misspelt or wrong word, and rewrite it, rather than scribble out one or two letters and insert one or two others. It is worth making sure that he knows where an insert goes; I have known boys who put it under the word instead of above it:
evry
  e

One further point. There are a few dyslexics who seem physically incapable of writing smoothly on the line. However hard they try, their letters snake on either side of it, yet their writing is perfectly legible. This may be due to a lack of fine motor coordination, and therefore out of their voluntary control, and it would thus be unfair to penalise them on that score. Such writers are easy to recognise, as their work looks as if it had been written on a jolting bus or train.

We must therefore, as teachers, insist on legibility, clarity and no ambiguous letters, but not necessarily on conventional letter-formation or artistic merit. It is worth noting that as confidence grows, and problems of poor reading and spelling lessen, writing does get better. If you can't spell or punctuate or make sentences, or read what you've written, why bother to make it look good?

Chapter 6

Writing

'True case in writing comes from art, not chance'
(Pope: Essay in Criticism)

In discussing dyslexia, a lot of attention is paid to reading (in the lay mind, dyslexia is still thought to be an inability to read properly), and spelling. Writing and speech come a poor third and fourth. And yet writing is a more creative and therefore more complex activity than reading or spelling. Through writing we attempt to convey our thoughts and ideas and what we have learnt, in a more lasting manner than through speech.

But we seem to expect that children, with very few tools other than some reading and spelling abilities, will be able to sit down and translate their thoughts into writing. That so many of them do manage to do so is a tribute to human adaptability. We as teachers of dyslexics have to offer more help than that. It's as if one were given pots of paint of many different colours, and brushes, and paper, and told 'there's all the equipment you need. Now make a picture'. Most dyslexic adolescents do not have an innate ability to write coherently; they seem unaware of what a sentence is, or of the function of the various parts of speech; they do not write in paragraphs, and they do not automatically see that the language they use for speech is not adequate for writing.

What do we all, as adults, need writing for? We need to write letters of application, messages and greetings. Personal letters, letters of sympathy or of complaint. We need to fill in forms, do

37

our tax returns, answer advertisements. We have to write cheques and envelopes, register at hotels, sign forms. We have to vary our writing style according to the situation, and be able to write consistently in capital letters if necessary. We need to write postcards to our friends when we're on holiday, and so on.

Additionally, during the whole of his school career, the dyslexic schoolchild is faced with exams and tests (nearly all of these written) and his greatest stumbling block is the English Language exam. It specifically tests competence in written language, and success depends on the one skill which he does not possess. If he fails to gain an English O-level, many doors are automatically closed to him, whatever his intelligence and ability.

Sentences

To achieve success in exams, and to be able to use written communication for all the purposes listed above, we have to start with the construction of sentences out of words. It is not always well understood what a sentence is; and once again, it is best if the pupil finds out for himself. It is a collection of words. Yes. It starts with a capital letter and ends with a full stop. Yes. Anything else? No. So we write down something like the following.

'Blue pink many green'. Is that a sentence? No. Why not? It doesn't make sense. Ah. So a sentence must make sense.

And so on. We end up with a perfectly satisfactory definition of what a sentence is, having had to introduce the words 'noun' and 'verb'. Noun is easy – a *n*oun is a *n*ame. But a verb is awkward – it's a 'doing' word, they'll say. So, is 'thinking' a verb? No, in their book, it isn't. It is easier to *show* what a verb is, than to explain it.

Thus: Jack and I _____ tennis together
        I _____ you are right.

Much practice with simple sentences makes the role of nouns and verbs clear. Adverbs then are simple: they are words we *ad*d to a *verb* to add to its meaning. But adjectives are not so easy to remember, because the word adjective doesn't link up with 'noun'. One of my pupils found the solution – he used the word adjective *as* an adjective – 'the adjective prefect gave me adjective detention' – 'adjective' being the unknown. (In this case, an acceptable expletive-substitute, presumably!)

By now, the pupil can make good sentences, using capital letters, full stops, commas sometimes, nouns, verbs, adverbs and adjectives (apart from pronouns, the other parts of speech only need a mention), and making sense. There is one more problem – unity, of tense and of person. What often happens is something like this:

> A hammer *is* a tool for hitting nails into wood, and *they are* made of iron and wood. People *bought it* in a shop.

In the course of less than 25 words the singular object becomes plural then singular again, and the verb goes from present to past.

Short, not Long Sentences

One way to overcome that problem is to aim for fairly short sentences. It is in the more complex sentence, perhaps with a relative clause, that the tenses and persons get muddled up. Curiously, it is not easy to convince pupils (or teachers sometimes) that short sentences can be just as effective and just as literate as longer ones. The 2 following extracts both use very simple English and fairly short sentences.

(a) Morning saw us over the Tunis Airfields. We were directed by a signal not to land where we had been told, and we were shifted to another field 40 miles away. We all got out, and they began to unload the baggage. It would be an hour before motor cars could come, and then a long drive. I felt completely worn out.[1]

(b) Ha was the first to call them. They hurried to him, and winced at the liquid mud that rose to their ankles. Liku found some berries blackened and left over from the time of fruit. Mel came and stood, frowning at the log. It was the trunk of a birch, no thicker than a man's thigh.[2]

The first extract is by Churchill, the second by William Golding – both winners of the Nobel Prize for Literature.

Some dyslexics experience severe problems in actually writing down enough words to make a sentence, and then linking it to another sentence. They tend to produce staccato groups of words which more or less stand alone. The technique here is 'step by step'. Take the word you want to say something about, and dress it – put clothes on it (not too many clothes – just the first layer).

Example (A) 'Dyslexia'
'I am a boy who has dyslexia'. Now say something else about dyslexia. 'It means that you can't read or write very well'. Now link those 2 statements so that you have one longer one.
    'I am a boy with dyslexia which means that I can't read or write very well'.

Example (B) 'rabbits'

1st statement	'rabbits are often pets'
2nd statement	'rabbits can be eaten sometimes'.
Final statement	'Rabbits are often pets, but sometimes they are eaten'.

If the subject you have to write about is more than a simple word (and it usually is), pick out the key word or words in the question or title, say something about them, and write them down.

e.g. young people waste their time in discos
Key words are 'young people'

1st statement	'Young people are always blamed for everything nowadays'.
2nd statement	'Young people like to enjoy themselves'.

Final sentence   'Young people are always blamed for everything nowadays, but very often they are only enjoying themselves'.

A lot of practice along these lines will soon lead to greater ease in expressing thoughts in sentences.

Paragraphs

Paragraphing is quite easily understood and is not difficult to apply. Now that rules regarding dialogue (a new line for every change of speaker) have been so much relaxed, paragraphs are a way of letting air into a dense wodge of words, giving the eye a rest, and breaking up the material into manageable portions. One has only to look at a page of printing without paragraphs, and compare it to one *with* paragraphs, to realise the psychological effect (especially on a poor reader) of the first. Also, paragraphs are a way of changing gear. One idea has been developed and discussed. Now to turn to another one, or another aspect of the first. I find that dyslexics only need to be shown *why* paragraphs are useful; they are then perfectly capable of using them. What they can do in practice, is to divide a page of writing into roughly 3 or 4 paragraphs. This has the added bonus of giving them a chance to stand back, and collect their thoughts. Going on and on without a visible halt seems to make them lose control – like a runaway train; ideas get muddled, tenses go haywire, sentences never stop, and they end up in a sorry mess. The sophisticated use of a paragraph, (perhaps only of one short sentence or phrase) to give a dramatic effect can also be shown, and adds to the dawning realisation that writing can perhaps be fun, that words and sentences can be manipulated to create a mood, or tension, or humour. Words are servants, the writer is the boss.

Essays

Almost certainly the most demanding, difficult and lengthy type of writing that most of us ever have to do, is an essay. The very name is daunting. Little children write stories – but older ones write essays (or SAs, as most dyslexics put it). The ability to pass any sort of English exam depends largely on competence in essay writing. The essay carries 40–50% of the available marks and is obviously considered to be of major importance. This bias is curious when one thinks that only a very small proportion of people ever need to write anything remotely resembling an essay once they've left school. But while the system remains as it is, and children have to write essays, so do dyslexics. They have to live in an essay-writing world, so we as teachers have to show them how.

The first task is to look at different types of essay and consider the pitfalls of each. In exams, there is always a large choice of titles, and they can be roughly categorised into

1. narrative
2. descriptive
3. pro and con
4. inventive
5. factual

(1)   The narrative essay is the 'telling a story' one. A typical one might be: 'Write a story with the following title: The man who dared'.

This sort of essay gives full rein to the imagination. A good story can be dreamed up about a mountaineer who has to rescue his injured leader etc, etc. The danger is, that as the writer plunges into his tale, and rattles off about the snow, the broken ankle, the heroic rescuer, he forgets the implication of the title – i.e. the man who dared would not normally be brave enough, but in this case . . . Also, in the general rush-along to get the story down, he hasn't thought *where* he's rushing to – i.e. the end of the story. So he finishes abruptly.

(2)   The descriptive essay often has a very short title, 'A rainy day', 'The view from my window'. The main hazard here I think is boredom. One really has to be able to write

extremely well, and with a good command of the less common adjectives, to make a success of such a topic. A cliché-ridden description of sodden trees will do nothing to gladden an examiner's heart, and moreover it's difficult to keep it going for about 500 words.

(3) The pro and con type of essay can look deceptively possible. Everybody has views about 'drug taking amongst the young' or 'School Rules – are they necessary?', but many people (not just dyslexics) have trouble in seeing the other chap's point of view. This sort of essay requires the ability to stand in someone else's shoes, and present a reasoned case for and against the argument. It needs careful organising, and a convincing tone.

(4) The inventive essay usually starts 'Imagine you were to . . .' or 'If you had won a holiday for two . . .', and it presents the same sort of problems as the narrative essay (1) – it is easy to lose sight of where one is going, and is difficult to end satisfactorily. I find that a lot of young people (not I think just dyslexics) do not find it easy to imagine themselves into an unlikely situation without losing touch with reality. The adventures suddenly become larger than life, the characters become epic, and the whole peters out into a confused fantasy.

(5) The factual essay is the type with a title such as 'Life at School', or 'Brothers and Sisters'. It offers an opportunity to write about something known and personal, and has the merit of being open-ended and unique. But being factual, one's feet have to be kept firmly on the ground. Wild flights of fancy and untenable sweeping statements are out of place here.

There is one other sort of essay, which *looks* like a narrative one, but is so full of pitfalls for the unwary that most dyslexics should I think be steered firmly away. This is the type which gives a few lines of a story then asks the candidate either to continue the passage, or to use it as the end of a story or description. This sort of writing is very hard to do well, for it demands that the *style* of the original passage be adopted. And not only the style – the tense, the length of sentence, all should marry well with the original.

Which Sort of Essay?

Having thus talked about all the different types of essay with your pupil, and knowing already what his strengths are, it is useful to decide which sort he is likely to feel happiest with. A few thoughtful and mature students can cope quite well with the pro and con essay, but on the whole, both that type and the descriptive type should be avoided. A dyslexic rarely has a large enough expressive vocabulary to do justice to a description, and even if he has, he tends towards an over-ornate and flowery style.

The clue comes from the pupil himself. It is striking to note how very haltingly and poorly most dyslexics write about subjects with which they are not familiar. But give them something to write about on which they and they *alone* are the experts – that is, themselves and their own experiences – and they can turn almost miraculously into fluent, compelling writers. And the best thing about writing about themselves is that many essay titles, especially the single-word ones, can be adapted to suit their own purposes. A boy who can write well about his experience of parachuting for the first time, for example, can use that experience to suit various essay titles such as:

'Saturday Night', 'The Non-conformist', 'A new start', 'The Challenge', 'Help', 'A friend in need is a friend indeed', and so on.

As there is always, in English exam papers, a large choice of essay-titles (for the CSE and O-level there are usually 9 or 10 to choose from) it is absolutely safe to assume that there will be at least one title to suit. The next job then is to practise and polish and practise again, writing essays on 2 or perhaps 3 subjects which the boy knows well. This will prepare him for essay-writing under pressure of time and examination conditions, and will give him confidence to tackle other writing.

This type of writing also fulfils that most vital of criteria – relevance. When we write about our own experience, we do so in a structured and sequential way. We are telling a story which is there ready for us to put down on paper – we don't have to wonder what happens next, or why, or who to. And isn't this just the sort of skill we need for most sorts of writing? What do you know about the life cycle of a worm? Describe how a slide-rule works. What were the causes of the French Revolution? All these questions require knowledge, yes. But given the knowledge, it has then to be written down clearly and in sequence. Which leads on to *planning* the essay. Even when you're writing about yourself, or have an experience to share, there must be planning. The subject has to be introduced, developed, and concluded.

Planning

There are 3 useful ways to plan an essay (or any sort of writing), any one of which will ensure that all the information or ideas you want to put over will be included, in an ordered way. Which plan is chosen will depend on the pupil's own preference, and sometimes Plan C can usefully be used in conjunction with Plan A or Plan B.

Plan A is a bubble or wheel chart, which is very familiar to most people, and more or less self explanatory. Assuming that the subject to be written about is 'Smoking', any ideas or facts about smoking are jotted down on the spokes radiating from the hub. These spokes are then numbered in order of importance. If several spokes seem to link together, they can be sub-numbered (1a, 1b, 1c, etc). Spokes can also be subdivided, or eliminated if they seem irrelevant. (See Wheel Chart on following page).

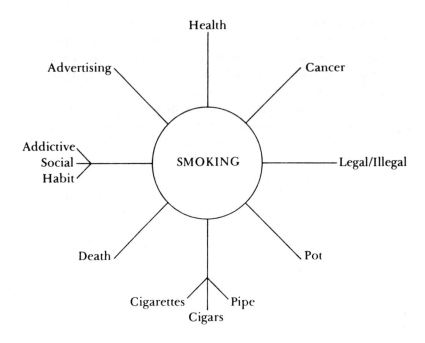

Plan B is a similar idea, but instead of spokes, one writes down any words or ideas relevant to 'Smoking' in a list. This is almost free-association – one idea or word triggers off another, so one might produce something like this:

cigarettes	tobacco	men/women
health	expense	social
dirty	legal/illegal	advertising
'pot'	America	sports sponsorship
cigars	Cuba	

Again, the ideas are put into a numbered order, and some may need crossing out. Yet others may occur, and be incorporated into the list – always making sure that they are to do with the essay-title, 'Smoking'.

Plan C –or the 'WH' plan, is both simple and very useful. It involves asking oneself all the questions beginning with 'wh' (including 'how', which does contain a 'WH'!). *Wh*at is it about? *Wh*o is involved/concerned? *Wh*ere is it happening/does it grow/ do people smoke? *Wh*en do they do it/did it happen/was it first introduced? *Wh*y is it important/pleasant/unhealthy/addictive? *Wh*ich issues are involved? *How* important/costly/dangerous is it?

Asking the 'wh' questions is catalytic – it makes you think, and it also ensures that you've remembered to deal with all aspects of the subject.

Plan C is particularly helpful when faced with other writing assignments or themes. For example:

Describing a hammer: What is it for, what is it made of, who uses it, why, where, when, how?

Writing about the American Civil War: What was it, who was involved, when was it, where did the action take place, why did it happen. How did it develop. What happened in the end?

This 'wh' method enables one to express in writing facts or ideas about virtually anything, from Biology to Physics, History to Car Maintenance or Dressmaking. Even letter writing can use the wh plan. Perhaps you need to write a letter of complaint. So, *wh*at are you complaining about. *Wh*y are you complaining? *Wh*ere did you buy it and *wh*en? *Wh*o did you speak to? *How* much did you pay? *Wh*at action do you want taken?

The Introduction

So now you have a plan. You know what you want to include, and in what order? So how to start?

The introduction, whether one sentence or a short paragraph, is probably the most important part of the whole essay because it is what the reader or examiner will look at first. It should therefore be stimulating, unusual, a little bit out of the ordinary. First impressions go a long way, and if you can catch the reader's interest, make him feel it's worth his while to read on, he may excuse a lot of subsequent clumsy phrases. An examiner has a very unpleasant job to do, and so it is well worth expending a little time and effort on pleasing him and making him feel positive towards you. The introduction could be humorous perhaps; or challenging and thought-provoking; 'Smoking is the opposite of cough medicine. Cough medicine is nasty but does you good, but smoking is pleasant and harms you . . .' It could start with a brief anecdote: 'After I had been caught smoking last week for the 3rd time, I decided . . .'

Whichever way one starts, it is a good idea to include the title word or words in the first sentence. It ensures relevance –the subject of the essay *is* going to be dealt with, right from the start. It also incidentally provides the actual, frightening first few words which are probably the hardest of all to put down. How on earth shall I start this essay? Look at the title again – what were the causes of the Irish Potato Famine? – so start 'The causes of the Irish Potato Famine are still troubling relations between Ireland and Britain to this day . . .'

The Conclusion

Ending an essay well is almost as important as the introduction. It need not be long, but nor should it be abrupt. A perfectly acceptable ending would be to re-state briefly the main points made in the body of the essay, perhaps adding some sort of personal recommendation ('in my opinion, smoking would be far less attractive to young people if . . .'). Be sure yet again to re-state the theme – it shows you haven't wandered from the point (too much!).

One more point. Take even more trouble than usual to ensure that the introduction and conclusion of the essay are spelt as correctly as possible; that words have their proper endings (no 's' or 'ed' omitted); that the sentences make sense and show unity of tense and person. As already mentioned, most people look first at the beginning and then at the end of a piece of writing. If they receive a favourable first impression, they are much more likely to excuse poor spelling and style in the rest of the essay.

Summaries

Summarising is another useful writing skill. All it really means is, saying what a passage/paragraph/chapter is about, and then briefly mentioning the main points. In a sense, it is the opposite of essay writing. Instead of being given a theme, thinking of all the things to say about it, and writing them down in a leisurely way, here one is being asked to *find* the main theme or point, look for all the supporting ideas relating to it, and write them down in one's own words as concisely and clearly as possible. And a very useful skill it is too, for most questions one has to answer in written exams in *any* subject, require just such a summary of one's knowledge on a specific topic.

Summarising is not easy to the uninitiated, and particularly not to the dyslexic, but there are 2 ways (at least) of helping.

(1)   the 'wh' plan works very well here. *Wh*at is this passage about? *Wh*o is involved, *wh*ere and *wh*en. *Wh*at happens? (Needless to say, not all the 'wh' questions are necessarily relevant for each occasion.)

(2)   Take a shortish, factual piece of writing, such as can be found in a newspaper or magazine article. Read it at normal speed to the student, telling him before you start that you want him to take one-word notes *only*, while you are reading. When you have finished, ask him first of all to tell you what the passage was about – in not more than 5 words. Then ask him to tell you the story back, with as much detail as he has managed to get from his one-word notes. Then ask him to write a brief passage, again using only his notes. With very little practice, he will soon be able to summarise quite efficiently. The next step is for him to read a similar passage to himself, and pick out the key-words or phrases which will give him the important points. He can either underline them or mark in the margin where they appear. He then has to put them together into a summary, using his own words as far as possible. It is very important to teach him always to ask himself, 'what is this about?' This will unfailingly give the key word or idea.

This exercise is useful, in that if it is done regularly in all his school subjects, he will be reinforcing his knowledge of a specific topic, and his notes or summaries will provide him with a valuable revision aid for exams.

More Techniques

For precision and conciseness in writing, three more techniques which I have found helpful are:

(a)   ask your pupil to describe in writing a common object without naming it – you will then try to guess what it is. The description must be such that any similar object is eliminated. Thus it would not be enough to write (of a chair). 'It is made of wood, and has four legs, and can be used for sitting' because this could also be a garden seat or a stool.

(b)   get him to write down as clearly as he can, in words, how to draw a simple shape, say a letter E, without using gesture or illustration. This is not at all easy – as is proved if you then try to draw what he has written!

(c)   tell him to describe a common object (e.g. a vacuum flask, using the following pattern:
      function (what's it for?)
      made of
      shape, size and colour
      parts

Summarising well is a most useful skill, and is worth spending some considerable time on.

Letters

Letters are a great favourite with examiners, and justifiably so, since almost the only sort of writing (other than form filling) which most people have to do at some stage of their lives is letter-writing. Letter-writing used to be dominated by all sorts of strange and archaic rules, so many dos and don'ts, that we are still anxious and apprehensive when writing, say, a formal letter accepting an invitation, or a letter of condolence. The rules have been somewhat relaxed recently, and we don't often see now such curious formulas as 'I am, Sir, your most humble and obedient servant', or 'I am in receipt of yours of the 8th ult'. My husband still remembers with pleasure receiving a reply from Hornby Trains to an order he sent them when he was about 10, which started off:

'Dear Sir, We thank you for your esteemed order . . .'

But even if letters are now much more straightforward, there are still certain formalities to be observed. These are explained in detail in books dealing with letter-writing, but there are several points to stress here.

(1)   Letter beginnings and endings cause endless confusion, and are moreover difficult to spell. They need to be learnt. A letter to a *named* person

   Dear Mrs Brown
   Dear John
   Dear Uncle Joe

must end with: Yours sincerely.
   A letter to an unknown person (Dear Sir/Madam) must end with

   Yours truly or
   Yours faithfully.

   Another useful spelling to know is 'affectionately'. (As recommended earlier, such spellings could be on a file-card in a wallet.)
(2)   Letters can and should be paragraphed, like an essay, and they should not end too baldly either.

(3)   Certain types of letters follow certain patterns, and I see no harm at all in working out together with your pupil a rough skeleton for, say, a letter of application, a letter of complaint, a letter of thanks, a letter booking a holiday, and a letter answering an advertisement, for example. Such skeleton letters would be immensely time-saving, and would provide the framework for practising.

(4)   A note about postcards. It is not always realised by a dyslexic pupil that the style and lay-out of a postcard differ from those of a letter. For once, full sentences can be dispensed with, as can the superscription and the formal ending, and the polite courtesies. I had a pupil once who had 0/10 for a postcard exercise, just because he *had* written it like a letter.

Checking Work

How often we wish our pupils would only re-read their written work before handing it in! And how futile that wish is sometimes.

We all see what we expect to see, or read what we *think* we've written, not what we've *actually* written. A dyslexic is no exception. Supposing what he writes is

'They men went shoping for beer and bun. The ask the shopkeepe were the pubs is'

Now ask him to read to you what he's written. Very likely he'll read it as:

'The men went shopping for beer and buns. They asked the shopkeeper where the pub was'.

There are dangers too in asking a particularly conscientious dyslexic to read over his work carefully, as he may quite easily 'correct' a correctly spelt word, and leave the misspelt ones standing in all their glory.

I am not suggesting though that no checking of work should be done – it must, but when? and how much? are the vital questions.

(i)   If possible, get a dyslexic to check his work after an interval – a few days, preferably. He will by then have forgotten what he actually wrote, and will come to it with a fresh eye. In an examination, tell him to check at the very end, and particularly the important bits (the introduction to an essay, for example).

(ii) It is not feasible to expect every word to be checked. But it is possible for any dyslexic to check that he has put a capital letter after a full stop; that he has put 'ed' endings on verbs if required, and 's' in plurals; that proper names have a capital, and that tenses are consistent.

(iii) If the pupil reads over his work *as if to a teacher*, he is sometimes able to spot quite a few of his mistakes.

Other forms of writing such as cheques, form filling etc. will be dealt with in Chapter 11 (Functional Literacy).

Notes

1. 'The Second World War', Winston S. Churchill (Cassell, 1950).
2. 'The Inheritors', William Golding (Faber, 1955).

Chapter 7

Speech

Speech is the real Cinderella of dyslexia. It is rarely mentioned in any text books on the subject, and most people are unaware that speech is implicated in the general problem.

But a word of warning. It needs dealing with delicately; very often speech is the only area of language in which a dyslexic has competence, so a heavy-footed approach is out. In fact many dyslexics, even adults, would say that speech has never been a problem, and for some no doubt this is true. But for others, speech is yet another area of language where they are uncertain of being right. Because of a poor vocabulary, they are not so fluent or quick in talking, and therefore they do not contribute so much to a conversation or discussion; they feel at a disadvantage in social situations and can be shot down in verbal arguments, so they become discouraged.

Our aim as teachers is to enable the dyslexic to convey his meaning accurately in speech as well as in writing. Usually when we listen to somebody talking we're not just understanding the actual words, we see the gestures, the facial expressions, we hear the tone of voice. All of these give us clues to understanding what he is saying. But if these clues are withdrawn (as for a blind person or on the telephone), and we have only the actual spoken words, it is immediately apparent that the average dyslexic does have a problem. He has a shaky command of grammar and poor vocabulary; he uses a lot of make-weight words (er, um, thing) and he doesn't speak in sentences (most of us don't always – but he doesn't, more than most). He mispronounces words.

Speech is important because

(1) it is the major means of communication,
(2) clear speech leads to clear writing,
(3) mispronunciations can adversely affect (a) understanding,
     (b) spelling.

And from a purely practical point of view – some Examination Boards require, in the CSE English Language exams, a part of it to be taken orally. The WJEC [1] for instance has an oral section which is worth 20% of the total marks, so increased competence in that area may make the difference between a Grade 1 and a Grade 2 (see Chapter 10, Examinations).

The help we can give is practice in speaking, formally and informally, until confidence grows and meaning is clear. Five or ten minutes every lesson spent talking with the pupil is time well spent, and if you refuse to understand him until he makes himself crystal clear, he will quite soon tidy up his speech (with some exasperation!). I sometimes say I'm a deaf foreigner who has to be made to understand – this eliminates mumbling and makes him seek for words to get the message over.

It is impossible to prove that tidy speech leads to better writing – but it is so. A pupil of mine was almost incoherent when he first started, and since he never stopped talking, meaningful communication was not great. I started interrupting him – sometimes at every other word (feeling very mean) – but he took the point, started to think, and was able within a year to express himself well. During the same period his writing too became fluent and well expressed, and he gained his O-level English last summer, at the second attempt.

Another example of speech affecting writing is the dyslexic who is the opposite of verbose. He has learnt early that people laugh at the things he says, or haven't understood him. So he takes refuge in silence; he becomes known as a man of few words, who answers in monosyllables and rarely speaks unless he has to. Inevitably then his written work will be very sparse too, and he will want to write all his thoughts down in as few words as possible. Such a boy needs his confidence restoring. Ask him to tell you about something he knows more of than you do, so clearly that you can repeat it back to him. Changing a tyre or re-wiring a plug are things I am not good at – so he can genuinely inform me by using the right words. This is a good morale-booster.

Tips

There are other tips for making speech more efficient.

(1)   You have your pencil poised over a clean sheet of paper. Ask your pupil to tell you in detail how to draw, say, a square. Something like the following may well occur.

    Pupil: Draw a line down.

So you promptly draw a long line from top to bottom of the page at the margin.

    Pupil: No, no, not there, and not so far!

    Teacher: All right, you must tell me. How far do you want me to go, and where do you want me to start?

    Pupil: Start in the middle of the page. Draw a line down for about 10 cms.

You start in the middle of the page as requested. But your line down goes towards the left for 10 cms.

    Pupil: (tearing his hair) No!

    Teacher: What sort of a line down, then? Horizontal? Vertical?

    Pupil: (with relief) Vertical.

And so on. Incidentally, in spite of the frustrations this sort of exercise is enjoyed!

(2)   Take a map, and get your pupil to tell you how to get from A to B, passing C, as

    (i)   a pedestrian
    (ii)   a motorist
    (iii) in a boat.

Mispronunciations

Mispronunciations can be amusing to the hearer, but embarrassing for the speaker. Some of these are due to childish habits not yet overcome ('v' for th, as in bovver), and should be worked on; a desire to leave childish things behind is a strong incentive.

Others are possibly due to insufficient reading or misunderstanding of other people's speech:

buttle (buckle)
aerial manager (of a bank!)
you better (you'd better)
addition and attraction (2 mathematical processes)
orgasm (instead of organism)

These spoken errors of course cause problems in spelling, and sometimes it is clear that a dyslexic does not always appreciate where words begin and end. This leads to written mistakes such as

alot
which ever
a mount

A boy I taught once was very familiar with the word College as it was part of the name of his school, and he had to write it weekly in his letters home. But when it came to the phrase 'Technical College' he seemed unaware that the known word 'College' was in it, and he both said and wrote it as 'technicolage'. This sort of mistake is not, of course, exclusive to dyslexics. The general public comes up with some marvellous spellings and mispronounced words: oberjeans, casants (chrysanths), pommie granites, were seen recently on a shop window.

Enlarging Vocabulary

Help in enlarging vocabulary can consist in:

(1)   Practice with synonyms and antonyms. Tell me 5 words similar in meaning to 'big'. What is the opposite of 'safe'?

(2)   Thinking of words suitable for describing a particular person, or a scene, or a sunny day, or the sea.

(3)   Finding words to convey different feelings: grief, anger, touching a peach, smelling a farmyard.

One advantage of having a poor vocabulary is that a dyslexic is not usually cliché-ridden, and he can sometimes find a very telling or apt word; 'proud' to describe a chandelier is one I remember. He is, though, very prone to use 'nice' and 'thing', and slang words which are not always appropriate to the occasion.

(4)   Working together at a sentence in a book or paper, and then putting it into other words, but still with the same meaning, e.g. 'Yet she seemed in some odd way contented' can become 'but she appeared to be strangely happy'.

Notes

1.   Welsh Joint Education Committee.

Chapter 8

Comprehension

Comprehension seems a curious aspect of language to offer help with. We tend to think that understanding is a product of intelligence, and that if it is lacking, nothing much can be done about it. But I think that in the case of a dyslexic, poor understanding comes at least partially from the fact that he is *used* to not understanding; he spends his life surrounded by people who use language to each other, and to him, which he is not entirely familiar with. He learns over the years (he's not stupid) to conceal this uncertainty – he's discovered that people become impatient with him if he's always not sure what they mean. So it's very important that we explain terms and technical expressions which we use, to him; that we constantly test his understanding of the language *we* use. It is no use talking about syllable-division and stress if he has only the haziest idea of what a syllable is.

He understands 'surface' language of course perfectly well, but he doesn't pick up information or new words or underlying meaning – they all need to be specifically taught. This is why he finds figures of speech difficult (metaphor, simile etc); why he can't read between the lines, or deduce someone's character or personality from a written passage. It is perhaps also the reason for the curious tendency he shows to ignore context when reading; if language in general is such a puzzle, with half-understood words, why not read:

'He could hear his father *tuning* in his bed' (turning)
or
'the room suddenly seemed too small to accumulate its 5
accidents'?
(the room suddenly seemed too small to accommodate its 5
occupants).

Context-guessing can be improved with simple examples. The
essential *logic* of language needs to be stressed, so that the pupil
gradually realises that 'not anything goes'. Made-up ludicrous
sentences are helpful:

(i)   She sat in the *flower* and warmed her hands in front of the
       frig.
(ii)   John and Peter went out *haunting* and shot two *peasants*.
(iii) I had meat and peas and *potteries* for the first course,
       followed by prunes and *customers*.

Another aid to help sensible context guessing is to select a
passage containing quite difficult words (a political report in a
quality newspaper is good for this), and ask what these difficult
words mean. Show the pupil how, by physically blocking out the
offending word with your thumb or a bit of card, you can read
the sentence and insert in the gap an appropriate word:

   e.g. You could rip a pin down the entire length and the delicate
       fabric remained unimpaired.

Block off 'entire' and you'll be offered 'whole' or 'total'.
Block off 'fabric' and you will get 'material' or 'silk'.
Block off 'unimpaired' and you may get 'O.K.' or 'all right', but
you won't get 'unimportant'.

Figures of Speech

Figures of speech are horribly difficult for a dyslexic to handle.
Simile seems fairly easy, because one can look for the words 'like'

or 'as' – but there are pitfalls in that, since both words serve functions other than to introduce a simile:

She was like a rag doll
but: She would *like* a weekend away.

Unfortunately, English language examiners are excessively fond of simile and metaphor, so exercises using very simple examples of both will at least make them more familiar and recognisable.

(1) 'The girls dance in the sun'
     'the waves danced in the sunlight'
     Do girls dance? – Yes
     Do waves dance? – no. So it means that the waves look like people dancing.
(2) 'His face was stormy'. What is usually stormy? The weather, when the wind blows and it rains and it's dark. So it means that he looked angry and dark like the weather on a stormy day.

Character and Reading Between the Lines

Because a dyslexic is often such a surface reader, he is slow to pick up unspoken implications and he tends to look only for the most overt, black and white, information. So if he is asked to describe the personality of a character in a passage, he may read it through carefully and come back to you saying he couldn't find 'where it said' – not realising that a personality or character comes through not only from what the actual text says about him, but from his words, his thoughts, his appearance, and from how other people treat him or speak about him. In the following extract, we are not actually *told* anything about the author but we can deduce a great deal.
    (From 'A Sort of Life' by Graham Greene)

I shared my bed with a multitude of soft animals of which I can remember a teddy bear (the most loved), a glove bear (it came second in my affection because it could not stand alone), and a blue plush bird (it was the age of Maeterlinck). I kept the bird, I think, only for the sake of filling the bed, because I disliked the feel of plush and I have mentioned my terror of birds. When quiet had fallen on the house, the fear of fire would emerge like smoke and I would imagine I had been deserted by all my family. I would drop the teddy bear out of bed and shout for the nurse or nursery-maid to pick it up. When one of them came, I felt assured again that all was normal, and I could sleep, though once I remember getting out of bed and sitting on the top of the stairs in order that I might hear the voices from the dining-room below, the low comforting drone of dull adult conversation which told me that the house was not yet ablaze.

It is helpful in this sort of situation to start thinking about how he (the pupil) *feels* about the person concerned – do you think he is a kind man? What makes you think that? What sort of age do you think he is? Would you like him if you met him? Why? Is he popular do you think, or is he a lonely sort of chap? Once again, a slight variant on the '*wh*' plan will provide all the answers needed to write quite a detailed character study of the person in question.

Chapter 9

Note-taking and Revision

After all the insistence earlier in this book on writing in complete sentences, expressing ideas carefully and with style – now we need to stand all that on its head. Good note-taking demands economy and few words, and is an absolute essential for successful revision.

On the whole, note-taking is thought to be a sophisticated skill, which the undergraduate will perforce pick up when he first starts attending lectures. But a dyslexic needs it long before that. Because his writing is slow and because he cannot take down semi-dictation quickly enough, the benefit he derives from some lessons is pretty meagre. He probably doesn't know the conventional abbreviations (not many people do), so he half-writes words in an illegible hand ending up with a page of 'notes' which are totally useless for any purpose at all. He can't read his writing later, he's forgotten what the half-words were, and altogether he's in a mess. Moreover, he's surrounded by his peers all scribbling away merrily and panic sets in.

So how to cope. Show him and teach him how to take notes (see Chapter 6, Writing). Read to him, but don't let him put pen to paper at first. Ask him what the read passage was about – the main idea or theme. That will be his key-word. Let him write it down, then read the passage through again, and tell him to write down (while you read at normal speed) more one-word ideas linked to the keyword. You then ask him to tell you what the passage was about, using his one-word notes. At this stage, he will see that some one-word notes need amplifying to give necessary detail.

Leave that piece of work for a week, then ask him to re-read his notes, and tell you the story again. He (and you) may be astonished at how much of the original story he can manage to reproduce. If there is difficulty in winkling-out the main theme and supporting ideas, the 'wh' plan will help.

Abbreviations are needed, too – but not too many. There is no merit in over-loading the memory with cf. or // etc. 'Therefore' is usually already known ($\therefore$) and 'because' is easily remembered too ($\because$). Ditto marks are a must, and the use of rudimentary {} to link like ideas is useful.

Words can obviously be abbreviated too and if the title is thereafter always referred to by its initial capital letter(s) (London – 'L', French Revolution, 'F.R.'), a lot of unnecessary writing is saved. (All these comments are self-evident to us; but not always to our dyslexic pupils.)

Revision

Dyslexic boys quite frequently come and say 'can you help me with revision?' The first thing is to find out how they actually do already revise – and pretty hopeless it is on the whole. There seems to be a totally unfounded confidence in the power of books to transmit their contents to the brain and memory of the patient reader, if he will just sit there with the book open in front of him.

It is quite hard to convince the pupil that this is not a reliable way of committing information to memory; a demonstration of the power and efficiency of note-taking (above) will usually help. This time of course, the pupil himself has to read, find the key word(s) and note the associated ideas, sometimes chapter by chapter, sometimes paragraph by paragraph, and here again (I apologise for being so repetitive) the 'wh' plan is invaluable.

The very act of writing down the main points helps to commit them to memory. If, a week later, the notes are found to be insufficiently detailed to give reliable recall, then the text needs to be consulted again for amplification. After 2 weeks, the notes alone should be enough for effective re-capping. If they are transferred to large sheets of paper and pinned on the study or bedroom wall, that is even better (or, alternatively on to file cards – perhaps a different colour-code for each subject – and kept in the pocket or wallet). Summaries done consistently during the year in all subjects are also ready-made revision material.

The actual lay-out of the page of notes is important, as very often one retains a memory of the 'look' of it, and one can then track down an elusive piece of information remembered for its position on the page. Anything that aids memory and understanding can be pressed into service – coloured pens, underlining of important words, or ringing them; arrows linking ideas, wheel-charts, numbered lists. (Don't forget numbering – it is a useful memory-prod if you've dredged up 4 consequences of the French Revolution, but know you had 5 written on your Revision Chart).

If long lists have to be committed to memory, (perhaps the names of different bones in the leg, or the names of some of the chemical elements) it may be possible to group them according to their initial letter, so as to make a near word or a memorable acronym.

*h*ydrogen
*o*xygen
*n*itrogen   }   = honc
*c*arbon

Chapter 10

Exams

Revising for exams is only half the story. The exams themselves need to be prepared for well in advance, techniques have to be learned and practised, and the special terminology of exams has to be understood and recognised.

By this stage, the dyslexic pupil will certainly have sat various exams and tests, usually set by his school. He will also almost certainly not have done very well in them, partially because many school exam papers are hand written by the subject teacher, and then cyclostyled or photocopied, resulting in a very variable degree of clarity and legibility. Dyslexics, who usually still read with some difficulty, are nevertheless accustomed to reading the *printed* word, and it seems unnecessarily unfair to burden them with the deciphering of handwriting, however beautiful. Exams are designed to test the candidates' knowledge and understanding, *not* to see how well they can read. It would be helpful therefore (to all candidates) if school tests and exams could be typed, and clearly photocopied.

Public exams, and the techniques required for them, are the main theme of this chapter. Whatever one may think of the examination system, and the aims of education in general, the fact remains that exams exist, and the passing or failing of them can permanently affect one's life and career prospects. So it behoves us, as teachers of dyslexic adolescents, to do our utmost to ensure that our pupils are well prepared and, by familiarisation, able to cope with the very special requirements and stresses of public exams.

The GCSE examination system, while having much to recommend it in theory (testing for understanding rather than parrot-learning, more course work, independent research, wider curriculum etc), does nevertheless present almost more difficulties for dyslexic students that the old O-levels/CSE system. Taking the English Language exam as an example, there is far more actual *reading* required in the paper, and as reading is still almost always considerably slower for a dyslexic than for his non-dyslexic peer, there is little time (or inclination) for re-reading – which can be a grave disadvantage, especially in questions requiring interpretation, such as the Comprehension sections. Sometimes reading is so slow and laboured that full understanding of a passage is virtually impossible.

The implications of a wider core curriculum may be such that a dyslexic student finds he has to offer for examination perhaps 6 or 7 'academic' subjects – whereas previously he could opt for some of the so-called non-academic ones – and he will therefore be landed with a very full timetable indeed, especially if he wants to offer the subjects he can shine in as well (Art, or CDT for example).

Course work or project work also causes problems for the dyslexic student, for 2 main reasons; one is that he is often poor at organising himself, and may have only a tenuous grasp of time-scales – a project to be completed in 3 months' time may well remain at the bottom of the desk till 7 days before deadline. Secondly, it is not easy for many dyslexics a) to read the material required for a project and then b) to filter or sift it to eliminate the inessentials, and finally c) to present it in a coherent and sequential summarised form. One of my own students spent an inordinate amount of time researching, taking notes, and writing a project on a comparison of Lenin and Mao Tse Tung for his History course work (to the detriment of his revision, and his other projects) – which was eventually marked out of only 7½.

Some examination boards offer the possibility of 100% course work in English Language. This may seem an attractive option, releasing the dyslexic student from the pressure of an exam. But it is not perhaps in the student's best interest to deprive him of the opportunities and skills required for timed, unprepared writing, as encountered in an exam. Life after school will certainly not offer many chances to prepare for thinking and writing in advance – letters and messages and memos have to be written as needed, and complex written messages have to be understood, frequently under pressure of time. Where the school does opt for 100% coursework, an additional exam in Basic English should certainly be considered. This exam tests for the ability to listen, read, understand and write, in everyday, relevant life situations.

Which Subjects?

For the dyslexic, some subjects to be offered for examination present more problems than others. English Language we have already discussed. Maths is very often a subject in which a dyslexic can shine – he usually understands the concepts perfectly well, and the paper contains very little written material to be read and understood. But there are 2 difficulties nevertheless:

1)   the dyslexic candidate will probably still be uncertain of his tables and computation will therefore be at best slow and at worst faulty. The recent relaxation over the use of calculators would seem to have corrected that problem, but calculators only work if the operator uses them correctly, and without the rough and ready self-checking ability which a knowledge of tables gives, errors will go unnoticed.

2)   reversal of symbols, to which any dyslexic may still be prone, especially under stressful conditions, can be fatal in maths exams. 25 misread as 52 will make the whole answer wrong, as will 969 written down as 696.

Any teacher who is preparing a dyslexic candidate for a maths exam needs therefore to be particularly aware of these two pitfalls, and to alert his pupil to them.

Most foreign languages are not a good idea for dyslexics. They all involve the use of symbols, and these symbols, though superficially similar to the ones used in English, usually mean something different, so confusion is inevitable.

For example, a Welsh dyslexic child writing in English may put 'mae dad' because 'ae' in Welsh is pronounced as 'y' (my) in English.

Oral work on foreign languages is possible though, and some dyslexics who enjoy languages can do well in oral exams.

Scientific subjects such as physics, chemistry and biology, are often perfectly possible for dyslexics to do well in. They require good understanding, rather than memory, and though a lot of the words used are very long, they are often phonetically regular and therefore comparatively easy to spell correctly, and can usually be grouped in 'families'. The snag is that most words *have* to be correctly spelled; one letter can alter the meaning fundamentally: (axis/axes; basis/bases; cyclohex*a*ne/cyclohex*e*ne).

For these subjects in particular, vocabulary work is both necessary and helpful – the most common and/or difficult scientific words can be grouped together on individual subject cards, and either kept handy in a wallet or pinned to the bedroom or study wall.

Subjects such as English literature, history, geography and scripture are often popular at the GCSE stage, but they can be tricky. They involve the accurate knowledge of place-names, people-names, titles and dates – an unwelcome load for the dodgy dyslexic memory – and they all require the skills of summarising and essay-writing. Sentences have to be newly-minted out of the head, and ideas and opinions have to be clearly expressed in writing. A great deal of continuous and regular work on presenting information succinctly is necessary for these subjects to bring success in examinations. A dyslexic with poor handwriting or imperfect motor control will also have difficulty in producing clean and accurate map work.

Which Board?

There are all sorts of problems, both administrative and logistical, involved in trying different Examination Groups for different subjects (or even just English), and they vary according to the school which the dyslexic pupil attends. But virtually all the Boards in the British Isles do have a policy towards dyslexic candidates, and it is well worth writing to find out what, if any, allowances are made, and also what each Board's exams consist of. Do they set conventional papers? or do they offer Multiple-Choice questions? Is it all coursework, or 50% coursework and 50% examination? Some Boards allow extra time (20 minutes usually), or the use of a published dictionary. Some allow the use of a scribe or a tape-recorder. Some allow the use of rough paper which does not have to be handed in.

Having found out what each Board offers, one then has to think carefully about the pros and cons of each allowance. Is extra time really beneficial, or is the pupil too tired anyway to take advantage of it? Does he have time to consult a conventional published dictionary for word meanings, or would a spelling dictionary (such as secretaries use) or a brief spelling check-list be more useful? One of my pupils came across the sentence 'he was apt to fire up', so he looked up 'apt' in his dictionary and found that it meant 'clever' or 'able'. The resulting confusion in his mind can be imagined, and he lost about 7 minutes of valuable time. If a scribe or a tape-recorder are allowed, the pupil needs an immense amount of skilled coaching, and a great deal of practice, if he is to do himself justice. Speaking into a machine or to someone else is *not* easy, and to assemble one's ideas and maintain some degree of fluency is a daunting task.

Again, multiple choice questions are not as straightforward as they might seem, and the nuances of meaning between 3 possible answers may be quite beyond a dyslexic's capabilities. Also the instructions for completing a multi-choice type of paper sometimes takes up a whole page of dense printing, and thus only aggravate the poor pupil's problems. Careful coaching and prolonged practice are called for here too.

A complete list of all Examination Boards, with their addresses, appears at the end of this chapter.

The Language of Exams

Now to turn to the actual exam papers. Before dealing with the techniques required, the language used in the paper is worth noting. Suddenly it seems a whole new vocabulary springs into action, using words and phrases which are not only unfamiliar, but which are rarely if ever used in any other context. For example, 'compare and contrast' or 'justify your answer'. The following are the 4 questions set on 3 linked passages about 'Concorde', in a WJEC CSE English language paper. To my mind, they are confusing, ambiguous and unclear and were indeed found to be so, and not only by the dyslexic candidates.

(a)   Choose any 3 statements made by the advertisement, extract A, and show how the information in the other extracts supports each of these claims.
(b)   Using extracts B and C only, explain any 3 of the main advantages of this aircraft.
(c)   Describe in some detail one of the major drawbacks of this aeroplane for the passengers and one for the pilots.
(d)   From all the information in extracts B and C, describe one major attraction or disadvantage of the aircraft which the advert, Extract A, does not mention.

Question (d) incidentally, was worth 2 points. The language used in these questions repays closer study. Why talk about aircraft in one question, aeroplane in the next? Is there any difference in meaning between 'describe', 'show' and 'explain', and if so, what? Is 'extract' (a) a verb or a noun? (It was thought to be a verb by one candidate at least.) Is 'statement' the same as 'claim' (a)? In (d), to link 'attraction' and 'disadvantage' with 'or' suggests similarity not difference, and was therefore read as 'attraction or advantage'.

Another ambiguous question reads 'Explain briefly both the main points which could be made in support of the development of motorway systems in built-up areas and the main points which could be made in argument against such a policy'. Does the word 'both' refer to the 2 main points? Or does it mean the main points for and the main points against?

Some of these linguistic ambiguities are easily accommodated by the non-dyslexic. And indeed the dyslexic, like the rest of us, will have to read documents, letters and official forms whose meanings are far from crystal clear. But our job is to make sure he too can learn to cope with the language which confronts him.

There are other language difficulties in exam papers which need explaining to the dyslexic candidate. One is the use of 'l' as an abbreviation for 'line'. For instance:

Explain the meaning of the following expressions:

a)   'show little distaste for prison life' (l. 4)
b)   'mutilation and outlawry were common in the Middle Ages' (ll. 12 and 13)

In (a) 'l. 4' was understood by some dyslexics as 1.4, and a couple of minutes are wasted looking for the context in line 1; similarly in (b) 'll. 12 and 13' was thought to be 11, 12 and 13.

Self-evident perhaps, but not to all dyslexics.

Another problem arises when questions are subdivided. Thus, Q. 3 may have 4 parts (a) (b) (c) and (d), and (a) may have 3 sub-divisions (i) (ii) (iii).

3)   a (i)   (ii)
         (iii)
      b
      c
      d

It is not always obvious to the candidate that he must label his answers using exactly the same symbols, and in the same order. In a question with 10 subdivisions, of which any 3 had to be answered, a pupil of mine picked out 3, (g) (c) and (j), but labelled them (a) (b) and (c). He got no marks.

Studying the Paper

It is very helpful for the dyslexic candidate to become well acquainted with exam papers, the size and shape and colour of them, the way the questions are set out. This will lessen the fear and strangeness of the actual examination situation. As in map-reading, where every map is different but the principles underlying it are the same, so in exams – every paper is different, but the format, size, colour and vocabulary used are familiar and recognised. As soon as dyslexic teenagers reach the 4th form, and have chosen their GCSE subjects, they can be introduced to actual papers. Not to do them at this stage, but to study the instructions, see how many questions have to be answered, how much choice there is. How long does the exam last? Should the time be divided equally between all the questions? Does it matter what order you do them in? (no – so long as you label clearly which question you're tackling). What about the marking? All these questions can be answered by spending a lesson or two studying a sample exam paper.

It is important to realise that much of the relevant information needed will be found at the very beginning of the paper; there is too often a tendency to turn over straight away to read the actual questions. But the front page will indicate a) the duration of the exam, b) the number of questions to be answered, and from which sections. It may also contain advice as to how long to spend on the main question, and it may tell the candidate what aids (dictionary etc) he may use. Then he should spend a couple of minutes looking at the marks available for each question. It is no use spending equal time on each question, if Q.1 is worth 20 marks, and Q.2 only 10 marks.

Sometimes one question may contain 10 parts (this is the case in Comprehension type questions in particular), and again, it is worth noticing which parts are considered more important. If a) carries 4 points and b) 1 point and e) 6 points, and time is short, do e) first and with greater care, then a). Leave b) to the end if there's time. The order in which questions are answered is at the candidate's discretion, *so long as* he remembers to indicate clearly which one he is answering. This cannot be stressed enough. If examiners wanted the questions answered in the order in which they were set, they would say so.

Now, and only now, should the actual questions be looked at. Here again, read *very* carefully any preliminary instructions, note any 'either–or' (real pitfalls), and any heavy-type or italics – these will certainly indicate that an important message is being conveyed.

Most of the above comments pertain to *any* exam paper. But one paper which almost every candidate has to sit is the English Language paper, so I make no apology for going into it now in greater detail.

The Essay

Because there is always, rightly, a wide choice of essay-subjects, there is also inevitably a lot of actual reading to be done, and for some poor readers there may be a problem of time. Here again, the dyslexic pupil should be alerted to look for clues. Quotation marks, for instance, will probably suggest that a discussion-type essay is called for. Question marks indicate that personal opinions are going to be required. A large chunk of print probably means that an essay has to be written in the same style as the extract. Probably the poor reader's best bet is to go for the single word, or short, title for his essay, because it will by definition be generalised, and therefore adaptable to many themes (e.g. Help. Fire. The Outcast. The Perfect Holiday). It can also be prepared in advance.

The Comprehension Question

The paper tends to say 'read the following passage carefully, and then answer the questions which follow'. And dutifully, the dyslexic pupil ploughs through a great wodge of print, *then* reads the questions which follow. It is more economical of his time to alter the order – to read the preliminary instruction carefully, *then* read the questions at the end of the passage, and *finally*, read the passage itself. In that way, he knows what he is supposed to be looking for, he can start marking the passage as he reads it when he notices anything relevant, and where there is a choice, he can more quickly eliminate that particular question.

The type of comprehension question which is particularly tricky for a dyslexic is the one requiring the replacing of certain words or phrases with others similar in meaning. Because of a poor vocabulary, he is frequently uncertain of word-meanings, but he can be taught to make an intelligent guess by physically (with a finger) blocking out the word, in its context sentence, and putting in an appropriate replacement.

For example, in the sentence (already quoted) 'the delicate fabric remained *unimpaired*', a pupil of mine, unprompted, looked at unimpaired and decided it meant 'having no pair'. When I encouraged him to block out the word, he was easily able to substitute 'untorn' or 'whole'. This blocking-out technique also guards against putting in the wrong part of the word, or too many words, which is a common error. For instance, 'gibbering' was translated 'like a monkey' – which would be quite good, except that the sentence would now read:

'In my panic, I started like a monkey'.

Or again, putting an adverb instead of an adjective is prevented by this method, so that in 'her punishment was richly deserved', richly should be replaced by a suitable adverb, perhaps 'well', not by 'good'.

Understanding the question clearly is of course essential – and some questions, as I have already indicated, are far from limpid, so the dyslexic pupils need a great deal of aided practice in teasing out what is actually meant, and in discovering what they are supposed to be doing. Two examples from a recent O-level paper:

(1) Using the whole passage as evidence, make an assessment of the young man which shows what, in your opinion, may be for and against his chances of getting another job.

(2) What is stated in this passage about the origin, composition

and behaviour of the moon which has not been proved and must remain as theory, assumption or estimate?

In the latter example, the question really asks 'what in this passage is not *fact* (i.e. proved) about the moon?' Therefore the key-word is 'proved'.

All this careful reading of the question and searching out the meaning may seem time-consuming, but it is surely far better to spend 5 extra minutes making sure one understands the question, than answering it wrongly.

The Letter/Life Skills Question

This often looks deceptively easy.

(i)   'Write a letter to your local newspaper giving your views on
       . . .
(ii)   Draw up a list of rules for . . .
(iii) Write a page of information about your town for a party of foreign children . . .'.

Absolute minefields, all of them, unless the candidate is able to present his arguments reasonably and cogently (for (i)); use the appropriate brief but clear style for rules (for (ii)); and write simple words and simple sentences in an attractive style (for (iii)). Only 10 marks are usually allocated to this sort of question – but they may make the difference between a reasonable grade and a poor one.

The panic factor needs to be taken into account. To be in a large room full of your peers, all busily scribbling away while you are still reading the questions, is not a reassuring situation to be in. The great temptation is to join them. This must be resisted if at all possible – I often feel horses' blinkers should be handed out to each candidate at the beginning of an exam; or ideally each pupil should sit in a small booth. But it is quite simple to demonstrate the benefits of careful, and unhurried reading of the instructions by the use of a small test. (This is best done in a group. I thank Lee Pascal for the idea.)

Put in front of each pupil, face-down, a typed list of simple questions, preceded by instructions. Tell them that at the word 'go' they are to turn their sheets over, read the instructions carefully, and then answer the questions. Tell them they will have say 4 minutes to complete the paper. Because of the panic-inducing aspects (timing, turning sheets over, being in a group), it will be a *very* small minority which actually follows the instructions as specified.

Lee Pascal's (adapted) list

READ ALL THE QUESTIONS CAREFULLY BEFORE YOU START WORKING

1.   Write your name in full

2.   Write your address in full

3.   Name 5 parts inside a car engine

4.   Write down the alphabet in order, in capital letters

5.   Write down the alphabet in reverse order, in capital letters

6.   Write down 5 words beginning with O

7.   Answer only question 1.

Oral work

Happily, oral ability is taken into account in the English Language exam, though in a less formal way than hitherto. It is still very important, though, that our dyslexic students are given training and practice in using oral language as effectively and clearly as possible, and in developing listening skills – which are often surprisingly inadequate. The reason for this may well be that some dyslexics 'switched off' at an early age, and have become used to not listening and not understanding.

Because oral work seems obvious and easy, very little preparation work is deemed necessary. But in fact, it pays rich dividends to prepare dyslexic candidates as carefully for this, as for the written papers. We have found that dyslexic boys have been able to score very high marks indeed, and have even done better than their non-dyslexic peers.

In a formal test of oral ability (other than the informal oral participation in classroom activities), a short talk may be required. This is a deceptively simple-looking exercise, but it can be a real hazard without some thought and much rehearsal. First of all a topic has to be chosen; this too often tends to be a cliché, such as rugby or football or holidays. I think the poor examiner needs to be considered here – having already heard half a dozen halting accounts of an exciting match, he will gratefully latch on to hearing about Hadrian's Wall, or an unusual hobby, or playing the flute. The theme chosen should be known, and known well, to the speaker; *he* is the expert, so he should not only interest his hearer, but be able to speak with ease and authority. It may be difficult for a 15 or 16 year old to have an area of knowledge or expertise, but that does not matter too much so long as he has an interesting subject ('Dyslexia' might be a happy choice). But knowledge and expertise are not enough to produce a good talk. As with written work, it needs to be planned and ordered, and the first phrase or two rehearsed – the actual examination situation may have a disastrous effect on one's thought processes at first! It needs to be informative and interesting and flexible enough to allow for interruptions or queries from the examiner.

Ignorance does not matter in this sort of talk – if for example the examiner asks about a technical detail, it is perfectly acceptable to say 'I'm afraid I don't know the answer to that one. But I can tell you about X'.

As with reading aloud, a clear delivery and confident voice are helpful. The deaf old foreign lady in the corner is useful again here – though this time she should face the speaker; he must become accustomed to being watched while he speaks, and to making eye-contact.

So far in this chapter we have concentrated on how to read and study an exam paper; we have pointed out the pitfalls, and discussed how to help prepare for an oral exam. But how can the candidate be helped when he is actually sitting in the examination room, he's read all the instructions carefully (we hope), and he now has to put pen to paper? In other words, how to start writing?

How to Start

A useful first sentence, to break the ice, is to rephrase the question. It may not be highly original, but it has the merit of concentrating the mind on the topic under consideration, and it enables a first line or two of perfect spelling to be produced (because all the words needed will be found in the question), thus giving a favourable first impression. This is important. If the examiner gets a good initial impression, he will view subsequent mistakes with more tolerance than if the first sentence were ill spelt and untidy. So for example the question might be:

'What were the main causes of the French Revolution?' and the answer might start:

'The main causes of the French Revolution were . . .' This makes it clear that the topic is the French Revolution, and the key word(s) is 'causes' or 'main causes'. At this stage a plan (p. 45) needs roughing out, listing the causes in order of importance, and a few brief, complete sentences should be written about each one. Short sentences are perfectly acceptable; they encourage clarity of thought and expression, and they ensure that persons and tenses do not become muddled up (as they tend to, in longer complex sentences). It is essential to keep referring back to the question – the candidate should learn to ask himself 'am I still with it?', and to use the 'wh' techniques he has previously practised – what's it about? who's involved? why? when? where? what happens? Ideally, he should then read over what he's written, re-read the question, and write a brief concluding sentence, again drawing. in the question – 'There were many causes of the French Revolution, but the main one was . . .'.

Set Books

Finally, a word about Set Books. These by definition cause great problems for dyslexic candidates. One answer is to use tapes. Many of the great classics, and the more recent popular novels and plays have been commercially recorded and although abridged they can provide excellent back-up support for the actual reading of the book. Books which do not appear on the commercial lists can be read on to cassette by the teacher, or by an interested parent. This is not too awful a chore and many people enjoy reading aloud. Additionally, it can be very helpful if the teacher reads parts of the book aloud in class, perhaps the beginning of each chapter, or a particularly complex section. This would stimulate interest and willingness to persevere in the dyslexic pupil, and be of benefit to all the pupils.

Examination Boards: Addresses

Northern Examination Association (NEA)

JMB   Joint Matriculation Board
         Devas Street, Manchester M15 6EU
ALSEB Associated Lancashire Schools Examining Board,
         12 Harter Street, Manchester M1 6HL

NREB	North Regional Examinations Board Wheatfield Road, Westerhope, Newcastle upon Tyne NE5 5JZ
NWREB	North-West Regional Examinations Board Orbit House, Albert Street, Eccles, Manchester M30 0WL
YHREB	Yorkshire and Humberside Regional Examinations Board, Harrogate Office – 31-33 Springfield Avenue, Harrogate HG1 2HW Sheffield Office –Scarsdale House, 136 Derbyshire Lane, Sheffield S8 8SE

Midlands Examining Group (MEG)

Cambridge	University of Cambridge Local Examinations Syndicate, Syndicate Buildings, 1 Hills Road, Cambridge CB1 2EU
O & C	Oxford and Cambridge Schools Examinations Board, 10 Trumpington Street, Cambridge CB2 1QB, and Elsfield Way, Oxford OX2 8EP
SUJB	Southern Universities' Joint Board for School Examinations, Cotham Road, Bristol BS6 6DD
WMEB	West Midlands Examinations Board Norfolk House, Smallbrook Queensway, Birmingham B5 4NJ
EMREB	East Midlands Regional Examinations Board Robins Wood House, Robins Wood Road, Aspley, Nottingham NG8 3NR

London and East Anglian Group (LEAG)

London	University of London Schools Examinations Board Stewart House, 32 Russell Square, London WC1B 5DN
LREB	London Regional Examinations Board Lyon House, 104 Wandsworth High Street, London SW18 4LF

EAEB   East Anglian Examinations Board
            The Lindens, Lexden Road, Colchester, Essex
            CO3 3RL

Southern Examining Group (SEG)

AEB   The Associated Examining Board
            Stag Hill House, Guildford, Surrey GU2 5XJ
Oxford   Oxford Delegacy of Local Examinations
            Ewert Place, Summertown, Oxford OX2 7BZ
SREB   Southern Regional Examinations Board
            Avondale House, 33 Carlton Crescent,
            Southampton, SO9 4YL
SEREB   South-East Regional Examinations Board
            Beloe House, 2-10 Mount Ephraim Road,
            Tonbridge TN1 1EU
SWEB   South-Western Examinations Board
            23-29 Marsh Street, Bristol BS1 4BP

Wales

WJEC   Welsh Joint Education Committee
            245 Western Avenue, Cardiff CF5 2YX

Northern Ireland

NISEC   Northern Ireland Schools Examinations Council
            Beechill House, 42 Beechill Road, Belfast BT8 4RS

Scotland

SEB   Scottish Examinations Board
            Ironmills Road, Dalkeith, Midlothian EH22 1BR

Chapter 11

Functional Literacy and Aids to Learning

Life, fortunately, is not entirely made up of exams, though to the dyslexic school child it must often seem so. To pass exams is very desirable, and the failure to do so may well affect choice of career or level of achievement. But in the final analysis, we as teachers would be failing our pupils very badly if we sent them out from school without the ability to function in the everyday literate world of adults. What does this mean? What do we all need to be able to do?

We need to be able to read notices, timetables, traffic signs, phone directories, instructions, the Highway Code, holiday brochures, forms, messages, menus, letters and newspapers. And we have to be able to decipher many different types of handwriting. We need to write (see Chapter 6, Writing) letters (personal, official, postcards), and letters of application; cheques, answers to advertisements, messages; we need to fill in forms, register at hotels, complete our tax-returns. We have to write in capital letters when asked to, and we need to vary our written language according to the need (a message to the milkman does not require the same degree of literacy as a letter of application for a job). We need to spell all the above as correctly as possible, and we need to know the alphabet.

No small order. To start at the end, with the alphabet. Not necessarily for dictionary work, but certainly for looking up telephone numbers. Most teenage dyslexics know the alphabet, as a rapid rate recitation. What they are not so good at, is knowing the relative position of each letter, and even reciting the alphabet to find where, for example, 'm' belongs, does not always work, as they pass it over without noticing it. The best plan is probably to provide a wallet size file-card with the alphabet written on it – in both capital and lower-case letters, for quick reference when needed.

Reading requirements vary in their degree of difficulty. A lot of road signs are predominantly visual and contain few words, so that on the whole they are fairly easy to cope with, given a modicum of time. But Helen Arkell tells the story of misreading a 'Caution' sign as Auction, and it is a good idea to familiarise the dyslexic pupil with the most common road signs and abbreviations – what does SLOW VEHS mean, painted on the road? and is M'Chester Chester or Manchester? We have to take in an awful lot of written information as we drive on roads and motorways nowadays, and the safety of all depends in part on how rapidly we can absorb and react to the warnings and notices we see.

Timetables and holiday brochures can be a daunting maze to the poor reader, and they are very often in minute print and dotted with footnotes. The dyslexic should be alerted to the use of asterisks, different colours, stars, boxed areas, heavy print – all of which indicate important information. Again, abbreviations – what is FB or HB? CH, SO, SX? (Full Board, Half Board, Central Heating, Saturdays Only, Saturdays excepted).

Newspapers present their own particular problem – because they are printed in columns, it is more difficult to achieve fluency in reading and thus maintain understanding (anyone doubting this should try reading aloud for a few minutes from a book, and then from a newspaper). Many words are perforce hyphenated, which increases their difficulty ('refer-ence', 'referrab-le', 'tip-ped' and 'express-ions' occur in one letter taken at random from a recent Guardian), and the style of writing is not always conducive to quick understanding. We are all familiar with the heading which is so condensed as to be ambiguous: Channel Tunnel Pronounced Disaster, is amusing, but it does typify the genre. As a young adult, the dyslexic reader may feel self-conscious and inadequate if he cannot discuss the latest news or soccer results with his friends.

Reading aloud is not exclusively a school-based occupation,

unfortunately, and later on in life the dyslexic may well suddenly be confronted with a reading chore: helping a friend to assemble a piece of equipment, perhaps from printed instructions, being asked to read the scribbled directions to a new shop, or being aked to read the minutes at a meeting. Many dyslexics resort to subterfuge – they've suddenly mislaid their glasses, or they haven't time just then. But it is well worth while maintaining reading skills and trying to achieve the slow fluency mentioned earlier. Menus are a nuisance, because of the tiresome convention of using French terms. The 'choose-for-me' gambit is probably the best here. There may be a few nasty shocks, but at least one won't be accused of being gastronomically conservative! It is important to realise that reading may never be fast or easy. But it can be competent, and often pleasurable.

The ability to write correctly is still a prized skill, in spite of word-processors and the telephone. Curiously, the more technical aids we dream up, such as cassettes, computers and word processors, the more we still have to use pen and paper. Forms have to be completed for countless everyday activities, and the sooner the dyslexic teenager becomes familiar with their format, and with the curious language of officialdom, the more confident he will feel. Sample forms of all sorts can be picked up in post offices or banks, or found in newspapers, and regular practice will enable him to become used to writing in capital letters, deleting as required, interpreting asterisks etc. Otherwise the filled-in form may be incomplete or unclear.

'I will/will ~~not~~ be attending the dinner on July 1st' was the response from a dyslexic ex-pupil received by a school which was inviting its old boys to a reunion. Was he wanting a ticket for the dinner, or not?

Writing cheques is another exercise which is more difficult for the dyslexic than one might expect. Writing the amount in letters is the awkward bit – does 18 have one 't' or two? How do you spell 40? – does it have a 'u'? A file card is called for again here. On it are clearly written all the numbers from 1–20, then in 10s to 100, then 1000 and (optimistically) 1,000,000. They are written in figures and letters, and on the reverse of the card can be written the months of the year. Some dyslexics are happy to use the 1–1–85 formula, but others are not so certain which number the month July is, for instance, so they need to be able to spell the month (or its abbreviation).

Writing out a cheque in the bank, or a shop, using prompt-cards, in front of a curious cashier or shop assistant may, understandably, not appeal to the dyslexic teenager. But it is usually possible to fill in most of the cheque in a quiet corner, and if pushed, a bit of fudging of the doubtful spelling will pass unnoticed. Most people write cheques very fast and far from neatly, and this is acceptable so long as the figures are clear.

Letters have been discussed earlier (p. 50), and the use of another file card for greetings and farewells. A sample lay-out for a business or formal letter might usefully be put on the reverse of this card, to provide a ready-made framework and thus save time.

There is much good and imaginative material available now to help teenagers (be they dyslexics or not) to acquire the necessary 'life-skills', and a short browse through a good bookshop should produce useful aids. The important point to remember is that such exercises must be relevant and topical. An out of date driving licence application form or an obsolete lay-out for a formal letter are definitely no-no's.

Aids to Learning

Apart from published materials, forms to practise on, and a few file-cards, what other aids are available to the dyslexic teenager (and his teacher) as he moves steadily up the school and prepares to go out into the world? Many dyslexia centres nowadays are full of splendid equipment, all designed to interest, teach and help the pupil, and many good ideas can be cheaply adapted to suit individual needs. At the teenage stage though, it is tempting to suggest that the only real essentials are pen and paper and some good books. (Good, in the sense of interesting or relevant. Not necessarily, or even usually, the classics.) But the following have been found helpful, to a greater or lesser extent, by most of our teenage dyslexic pupils.

(1)   Since b and d are still confusable, especially under stress, they can be printed or written on a ruler, a pencil case or even, in extremis, on the wrist. This will save worry and time.

(2)   For helping with mathematical calculations; a table square pinned above the desk, or a pen which shows the tables from 2 to 9 at each click of the retracting mechanism. Otherwise of course, calculators or sliderules (remember though the dangers of number-reversal).

(3)   A personal dictionary. This can be a small address-book, where the letters run vertically down the right hand side of the page and are clearly visible. In it will go any words which the pupil finds tricky to spell, or which he consistently mis-spells. Or words which he needs for a particular interest or topic. The awkward bit of the word should be underlined in colour, e.g. general. These words are *not* for rote-learning. Gradually, as the dictionary is referred to and used, they will become familiar and absorbed.

(4)   Subject-vocabularies. These can readily be compiled from past papers or text-books, and the subject teacher may be able to provide other words. The pupil can use any spare moments to practise them, or to learn the difficult ones which don't follow the normal patterns (protein, for example). Each subject should fit onto one side of a card and be colour coded, and either stuck on the wall, or added to the wallet-collection. Or they can be written in the back of the personal dictionary.

(5)   Tapes have already been mentioned, for helping with set books in English. They have a role too (if there is a cooperative parent or relative available) in other subjects; important chapters of text-books, or prepared summaries could be put on tape, and used by the dyslexic as revision aids. Tape recorders can be used by the poor reader, to practise and check on his reading aloud.

(6)   Typewriters and computers. Some dyslexics like using these, but others hate them. For those interested, typing can be surprisingly useful for improving spelling. Having to think which key to press next seems to encourage better

letter-order, and seeing it appear so neatly makes the spotting of errors easier. Because letter-formation is automatic, and doesn't need thinking about, the pupil has greater opportunity to concentrate on *what* he wants to write, rather than *how* to, and so the meaning becomes clearer.

(7)   Some teachers are willing to provide photocopies of the notes they use. These would have to be typed of course, and would supplement the actual lesson. Taking notes from the board or dictation is virtually impossible for the dyslexic. He tries to write fast, abbreviates meaninglessly, and mis-copies from the board, and his writing becomes illegible. I have had a pupil come to me straight from a History lesson where the class had had to take notes. Even so soon after the event, he was totally unable to reproduce anything useful at all, and because he had been concentrating so hard on actually *writing*, the meaning had become lost.

(8)   Class teachers could also be encouraged to provide details of where information can be found. Which book? Which pages? Where in the library should the book be? It is not easy for a dyslexic to 'skim' through rows of books, so the title and author should ideally be written out clearly on the board, and *left* there for more than 10 seconds. If homework or prep is written up at the *beginning* of a lesson, the dyslexic stands a better chance of copying it down correctly.

(9)   Dictionaries. As mentioned previously, the use of a dictionary for word-meanings is sometimes not very successful. Of more practical use for everyday is a Spelling Dictionary, which is much more concise, and has the added bonus of giving every part of a word under the one heading. So the entry for 'travel', gives 'travel, traveller, travelling, travelled'.

But possibly the very best aid for a dyslexic teenager is individual attention, even if only for one lesson a week, when problems can be raised and specific help given. In a recent survey of adult dyslexics, one of the questions asked was whether individual lessons had been interesting, relevant, and helpful. Many respondents had found them relevant, and most had found them interesting. But all, without exception, had found them helpful.

A final plea. We always need to remember that a dyslexic teenager, however able, will never be a faultless speller. He will almost never be a fast reader, and he may not be a rapid or neat writer. So we must not try to achieve the impossible – or let the pupil think he can. We must look for, and encourage, any sign of improvement, and indeed we should expect it. But underlining all spelling errors has no value, and nor has writing a word out three times – the third time it will very likely be mis-spelt again. Please do not:

(1) ask a dyslexic teenager to read aloud in public, unless he volunteers.
(2) ask for vast quantities and a complex style in written work. Do encourage a simple prose style, and an adventurous use of words.
(3) expect copying from the board to be correct or fast.
(4) write comments on his work which he can't read!

Please do insist on:

(1) full stops and capital letters – always.
(2) question numbers written down, and work dated.
(3) titles and headings for work.
(4) writing in to the margin, with a consistent slope.
(5) paragraphing.
(6) *logical* spelling, at all times.

Ideally, we should instil into our pupils an honest self-knowledge of their limitations and difficulties, but also confidence in their own ability to achieve and to improve.

Chapter 12

Epilogue

In this final chapter, some teenage dyslexics speak for themselves. The first 2 pieces appeared originally in the school magazine, so the spelling has been corrected. The next 3 are as I received them, except that I have occasionally put a word in brackets to clarify the meaning. Of the 5 boys whose work is represented here, all are of above-average or high ability and all have had individual help once a week for 45 minutes, for at least 2 years.

(1)   has 7 O-level passes and is studying for his A-levels. He has sat O-level English Language twice, and his last mark was a D. He is still trying.

(2)   has now left school, and is studying for some A-levels at a Technical College. He is still trying to get O-level English.

(3)   is currently working for several O-levels, having gained some CSEs last year. He has not yet passed the O-level English exam.

(4)   is very severely disabled by his dyslexia and his literacy skills are not adequate for any English exams as yet. He is nonetheless expected to get 5 O-levels this year, and is particularly good at Art and Computer Studies.

(5)   is sitting various O-levels and CSEs this year. He should eventually pass O-level English.

The final page shows three spelling lists. The last 20 words of the Schonell Spelling Test were administered to 2 dyslexic boys, and 1 non-dyslexic girl. All 3 are of above average ability. These 20 words are supposedly spellable by the average 15 year old. It will be seen that nearly all the misspelt words are nonetheless spelt logically.

(1) Written by M.G. (age 16) Spelling corrected.

After I had spent a lot of time looking up a list of words which I thought I would need for my essay and then putting my Cassell's spelling dictionary away, I cleared a space on my desk by removing books, papers, and milk cartons. I got my spelling sheet and placed it carefully at the top of my desk and well away from my cup of coffee because coffee gets spilt very regularly around my study area and it is very rarely me who spills it.

I then realised that I had no paper to write upon. I rustled around in my pile of papers which I threw on to the floor to make space for the paper. I eventually found a couple of pieces of paper for the essay. I then got started on it. By the time I had got to the fifth or sixth line a few more people came in to my study and started working for their free lesson. As I reached about a page and a half, the lesson ran out; the bell for the last lesson had just gone and I was about half way through the essay when somebody who had been revising for one of Mr. Lloyd's Chemistry tests walked past and tripped over my pile of books and hit the corner of my desk, causing my coffee to go all over my spelling sheet. Luckily I managed to get my essay out of the way. Feeling very pleased with myself I then wiped up the mess and carried on, only to find myself repeating myself. So all the joy of saving my essay was now filled with anger and from then on, when I started rewriting my essay, I realised that I did not have my spelling sheet with me any more, but I struggled on, trying to write my essay and trying to spell the words correctly which is nearly impossible to do with all the rest of the things to think about, because I am Dyslexic.

After struggling through most of the essay, I went back to the beginning and tried to read the mess of the ink on the paper I had left behind me. As soon as I started I was confronted with a word which was spelt so badly that I could not read it. After a long discussion with the whole study, I realized that I had spelt it back to front. Then I continued to correct as many spelling mistakes as possible and to punctuate it as well.

By the time I had got to the end of my corrections, much of the writing had been crossed out and rewritten above. I was feeling depressed, annoyed, and I felt like ripping the thing up into shreds.

Eventually I finished the essay, which was about 3 pages, an astronomical amount for me. It looked impressive in length, but not in appearance . . . good for me. I ran up to the staff room, put the essay in the pigeon hole with my apologies that the essay was a fortnight overdue.

(2) 'English, English!'

English is my native tongue and British is my nationality. I was born and bred in Britain, yet I still do not have my English 'O' level. Many of my friends are foreign, both in language and in culture, yet they have all passed English. So why can I not pass an exam without which my other exams, including 'A' level Maths and Physics, are virtually useless.

I will leave school at the end of this year to go forth and find what is gold to a gold-miner, a job. My goal is made even harder since officially I am not able to communicate to a high enough standard.

Why is it so difficult for me to pass my English? When I hand in exam papers, which I have done in my own time, I receive a pass mark every time. Sometimes I am given 'B' grade, yet in the actual exam I fail, mostly with a 'D' grade, but sometimes an 'E' grade. Some people say that my dyslexia is the cause of all my trouble. Before the word dyslexia was used to explain why many people could not read or write properly, you were just plain thick – and that was that. Well what has changed? When you have to read aloud you never volunteer to read. To a group of people you are not going to say that you are dyslexic, due to embarrassment. No, you just stand there, go red when you get it wrong and at the end you sit down and feel relieved. Meanwhile everybody else feels sorry that you cannot read properly.

Practice is one way to overcome a problem – but does it work for English? To practise English is for me one of the most difficult things. Maths and Physics are easy compared to English. They consist of set facts which do not change, but English is constantly changing. The exam has always the same four types of questions, but the ideas and attitudes can change. You cannot go into an English exam and know what sort of questions you are going to be asked. I have tackled my English exam in several different ways, but still no luck. Spelling is my weakest point. All spelling is is a few rules, which I know, and a memory, which I do not have, so why is it so hard to spell? I read books all the time, but my spelling has improved little in the past two or three years, so again, how do I solve the problem?

I have tried several different techniques in order to try and pass. It is amazing to what lengths you might go to pass an exam. I have started at the beginning of the paper and worked through, or started at the end and worked backwards. I have even tried going to sleep in the middle of the exam to try and freshen my mind. My dyslexic probem is the inability to correct a mis-spelt word. I also miss out or write the wrong word, so as the exam goes on, as three hours is a long time to sit in a chair and write, I become tired and so make even more mistakes. One tactic was to try different Boards but unfortunately that did not work either. At one point I decided that the entire exam structure was bad since I got better grades on the London Board than on the Welsh, yet if I had passed on the London Board I would still have an English 'O' level, but it would have been easier to get than the Welsh one.

I think the only thing I can do is to keep trying. One day I will get my English but until then I will be carrying a ball and chain.

A.L.

(3) Dyslexia

Dyslexia affects me in meny ways good and bad.

The disadvantages: makes my English a lower standerd than most people my age.

One of my meny faluts (faults) is mixing my words up and jumping letters. this affects my reading and spelling and writing.

Reading aloud is one more of my major difficultys. Peaking (speaking) in argue ment is not one of my strong points either because My words come out jumbled.

You have to revise harder and still not get as far as others

Peole say you arn't as bright because you can't read or spell briliantly

The advantages: arnt that meny but you have a simpathy for others how (who) have problems and you can cope with problems others wouldn't know how to handle

The advange I am not sure about is you are sopposed to have more common sence.

E.P.M.

(4) Being DYSLEXIC

it is not much difrent being DYSLEXIC apart from that you can not spell very well and if your a bad Dyslexic you are not very fast at reading. But all it means in the end is that you have to get a job out side an ofise. One very bad thing about being deslick is that people do not under stand that it is a dicbility they just think you are thick, and it is a way out. But on the games side you are just as good at playing. There is no difrence if you are (dyslexic) or not you live the same life as aney other person.

F.O.S.

(5) Dyslexia (extracts from a long account)

To me, dyslexia has always been rather more than a spelling problem. To me it has been more of a phisciological (psychological) one. It started when I went to a Prep School to board at seven. I found that very tough . . . it has a very high Academic standard and is tough, very tough, I belive it was a school where to suvive happily, you had two be intelligent and defintly not dyslexic.

The Headmaster . . . self-admittedly belived Dyslexia was a lacyness, and it was most deffinatly not belived in at the school. hopless . . . when your work was bad, mispelt, as was always the case with me, by the end of the lesson I was in tears. Once a week we had a grammar test, been (being) dyslexic I used to find it impossible to learn, especially it been a forgein (foreign) language. During my 3 years there I passed one and that one I cheated.

Each lesson I dreaded like my death. Slowly I was persuaded I was a lasy fool, and I of course excepted (accepted) it and lost confidence in myself completely, I thought I was stupid, all my lessons went downhill. The one thing that kept me going was that I had exelent freinds . . . my work was awful. Every two weeks we got an industry card, from each lesson we got a mark out of 2, the whole thing was out of 12, I genrely got Minus 4. Soon I got so destressed I began to cheat, and cheat in everything I did, life seemed so much simpler and happier . . . at the age of eleven they (his parents) took me away. It is a very good school in its way, but soul destroying for dyslexics. . . . I was sent to a school in the Wye Vally . . . it was all geered up for dyslexics and to my amasement I found I was no Idiot but top of the form in my first term. I was very happy there . . . they made me into a person again. The next year we played my old Prep School at Rugby beating them 50–0, to me it was a very Special victory.

T.R.

Spelling List

permanent	permannent	x	permenant	x
sufficient	sufficent	x	sufficiant	x
broached	broached		brocht	x
customary	customary		customary	
especially	esspecially	x	esspecially	x
materially	materially		materialey	x
cemetary	x cematry	x	cemetary	x
leisure	leasure	x	lesure	x
accredited	accrederted	x	acreditted	x
fraternally	faturnally	x	fraternally	
subterranean	subterrainian	x	subteranien	x
apparatus	apparatus		aparatus	x
portmanteau	portmantoe	x	portmanteau	
politician	politicion	x	polotition	x
miscellaneous	misurlanious	x	missolainious	x
mortgage	morgage	x	mortguage	x
equipped	equipped		equipted	x
exaggerate	exagerate	x	exadurate	x
amateur	amatur	x	amature	x
committee	comitey	x	comittee	x

19/20	5/20	3/20
Girl age 16^{9}/12	Boy age 15^{11}/12	Boy age 15^{6}/12
Not dyslexic	Dyslexic	Dyslexic
I.Q. 130+	I.Q. 140	I.Q. 120+

Book List

This is not in any sense a comprehensive list, but it does include many of the books which I have found helpful. In the 'Reading for Pleasure' category, I have only included *one* series of abridged books, as most of the others fail to give pleasure, due to line-numbering, and over-curtailment of the plot.

An excellent leaflet on examinations was produced several years ago by Margaret Newton and Michael Thompson of the University of Aston, Birmingham ('Dyslexia: a guide to Examinations'), and the Tayside Dyslexia Association (Dept. of Education, University of Dundee) has published a series of Information Leaflets, of which nos. 2 and 3 are particularly relevant (compiled by Catriona S. Collins, George Watson's College, Edinburgh).

General

BBC Adult Literacy Handbook (BBC 1975)
BBC Writing and Spelling Handbook (BBC 1979)
A New English Course (O-Level) *Rhodin Jones* (Heinemann Educational Books 1975)
    New English Third: *Rhodin Jones* (Heinemann Educational Books 1980)
        Fourth: *Rhodin Jones* (Heinemann Educational Books 1980)
Signposts to Spelling: *Joy Pollock* (Helen Arkell Dyslexia Centre 1978)

English Language: Penguin Passnotes: *Jill Talbot* (Penguin Books 1984)

Rapid Revision Notes. O-Level. English Language: *D.C. Perkins* (Celtic Revision Aids 1983)

Keyfacts – Course Companions (GCE O-Level and CSE) in various subjects (Intercontinental Book Productions)

Pan Study Aids: English Language O-Level and CSE Revision Cards by *P. Cloke* (Pan Books 1985)

Work Books

Passages for Comprehension: *P. Cloke* (Wheaton [Pergamon Press] 1980)

Three Ways to Comprehension: *John P. Jenkins* (Wheaton [Pergamon Press] 1980)

Developing Skills: *L.G. Alexander* (Longman 1967)

Words Work: *Joyce Nolan* (Oliver and Boyd 1978)

Spellbound (2 vols): *Elsie T. Rak* (Better Books)

English Language Study and Revision: *J. Macfarlane* (Collins Educational 1983)

Dictionaries

Hamlyn Good Spelling Dictionary (Hamlyn 1979)

Dictionary of Contemporary English (Longmans) (this contains sample sentences and phrases showing how words are used in context)

Spelling Check-List: Dictionary for Dyslexics by E.G. Stirling (St David's College, Llandudno 1984)

Reading for Pleasure

'Bulls Eye' Series ed. by *P. Nobes* (Hutchinson 1979 to present)
'Lives of the Great Scientists' etc (Ladybird Books)
Books by   *Gerald Durrell*
           David Nobbs ('The Fall & Rise of R. Perrin')
           Sue Townsend (The Diaries of Adrian Mole publ. by Methuen 1982 and 1984)
           Michael Moorcock (Science Fantasy Books Fontana 1980s)
Cassell 'Banjo' Books (30 pps) various authors (Cassell 1975 to present)
Databank Books by *D. Crystal and J. Foster* (Edward Arnold 1981 to present)
Fighting Fantasy Gamebooks: *Ian Livingstone and Steve Jackson* (Puffin 1983) (using dice, pencil and paper)

Notes

Notes

Notes

Notes

Notes